PUFFIN BOOKS

THE ULTIMATE MEMORY HANDBOOK
FOR STUDENTS

Aditi Singhal and Sudhir Singhal, founders of Dynamic Minds Group, are international memory trainers, mathematics educators, authors and motivational speakers. They hold the Guinness World Record for teaching mathematics to the largest group of students.

Aditi has also been given the Best Memory Trainer award by the India Book of Records and has been featured in *The Limca Book of Records* thrice for her memory and fast calculation skills.

Together, Aditi and Sudhir have authored three bestselling books: *How to Become a Human Calculator, How to Memorize Anything* and *How to Be a Mathemagican.*

'I was introduced to these wonderful techniques through one of the authors' YouTube videos. I was impressed with the simplicity of their explanation. Along with the memory techniques, I found their scientific revision plan very unique and useful. I encouraged my daughter, who was in the twelfth standard, to try these methods. The revision plan helped her make an organized schedule and the memory techniques taught her how to retain everything she had studied. I am glad that the authors have written this book'

—Arti Saswadkar, Mumbai

'Classes with Aditi Ma'am and Sudhir Sir used to be the best part of my day! We had so much fun, and the tricks and tips they taught us played their part in improving our memory. It's been more than nine years since I trained under them, yet those lessons are as fresh as ever in my mind. They helped me not only in school and college but also in my professional life. Thank you, ma'am and sir, for helping us use the right and the left parts of our brain together'

—Priyapreet Kaur, company secretary, Delhi

'I was exposed to the incredible world of memory techniques at the tender age of twelve, during a workshop run by Aditi Ma'am and Sudhir Sir. The tips and tricks I learnt then have been my stable companions over the years and have now become second nature to my learning processes. They are easy and fun ways of smart memorization that enhance understanding and recollection. It is remarkable how these techniques remain just as relevant in university as they were in school. Kudos to Aditi Ma'am and Sudhir Sir for sharing this wonderful discovery with the world!'

—Mehvash Saiyed, former head girl and 2018 humanities topper, Delhi Public School, R.K. Puram

THE ULTIMATE
MEMORY
HANDBOOK FOR
STUDENTS

ADITI SINGHAL | SUDHIR SINGHAL

ILLUSTRATIONS BY M. SAQUIB

PUFFIN BOOKS

An imprint of Penguin Random House

PUFFIN BOOKS

USA | Canada | UK | Ireland | Australia
New Zealand | India | South Africa | China

Puffin Books is part of the Penguin Random House group of companies
whose addresses can be found at global.penguinrandomhouse.com

Published by Penguin Random House India Pvt. Ltd
7th Floor, Infinity Tower C, DLF Cyber City,
Gurgaon 122 002, Haryana, India

Penguin
Random House
India

First published in Puffin Books by Penguin Random House India 2018

10 9 8 7 6 5 4 3 2 1

ISBN 9780143442851

Typeset in DIN Next LT Pro by Manipal Digital Systems, Manipal
Printed at Thomson Press India Ltd, New Delhi

www.penguin.co.in

MIX
Paper
FSC FSC® C010615

To the
Almighty God,
the supreme father of all souls and
the source of true knowledge

CONTENTS

★★★

PREFACE

Encouraged by the amazing feedback from the readers of our book *How to Memorize Anything* (Random House India, 2015) and from parents who are deeply concerned about the academic pressure their kids face, we offer you *The Ultimate Memory Handbook for Students*. It is a complete manual for school students to learn and apply memory techniques to their academic curriculum and attain unparalleled success in subjects such as science, mathematics, social sciences and even English.

The current learning methodology falters in differentiating between studying and learning. The main idea of educating oneself gets lost in the melee of performing well in exams. Students are told what to learn but are not empowered with the right skills to do it; so, through trial and error, they try their own methods to cover their coursework and eventually lose interest in gaining knowledge. Good scores seem to be the only aim.

The result is for all to see. Once a child is out of school or progresses from one grade to the next, they forget what was learnt in the past.

It's not just kids—we grown-ups also feel that most of what we learnt is now outdated or irrelevant. But this is not true. We don't practically use the knowledge gained in school as we don't remember it any more. That's why it is important to start learning things the right way from the beginning. Although memory techniques are useful for people of all ages and professions, it is most beneficial to students.

Information stays with us forever only if it is registered in the right way in our brain.

✓ Won't you feel nice if the things you learn stay with you forever?
✓ If you remember the names of all the bones in your body even when you are sixty?
✓ If you don't need to refer to Google to check state or country capitals?
✓ If you instantly remember the meaning of a word years after you read it in a newspaper or a book?
✓ If you know important historical dates like the back of your hand?

If your answer to any of the above question is yes, then this book is for you.

The techniques in this book are interesting, practical, fun and easy to understand. It is only by using these memory techniques that we created a Guinness World Record for conducting the largest math class, helping 2312 students memorize multiplication tables till ninety-nine.

While going through this book you will be surprised to see that you have been using some of these techniques unknowingly. We have been teaching these memory techniques to school teachers and students for a long time. By popular demand, we are happy to present these student-friendly memory techniques in this book.

There are two sections in this book. In the first, we explain, in brief, some basic and advanced memory techniques with suitable examples to understand their usage. The second section is further divided into different subjects, where we have taken questions directly from the school syllabus, like the

National Council of Educational Research and Training (NCERT). Here, memory solutions are given using various combinations of techniques taught in section one. We recommend that you go through the first section thoroughly in order to understand the second.

The principles for learning or memorizing anything remain the same irrespective of the subject. For example, the techniques used to memorize long history answers are also applicable to other subjects. How we memorize numbers remains the same, whether you must remember history dates, physics constants or the periodic table. In the same way, the method used to learn English vocabulary or foreign languages also helps us memorize different scientific terminologies and important general knowledge. There are a variety of applications of a single technique across subjects. So, we suggest that you read the examples given for all the subjects to have a better understanding of the application of these techniques.

Most of the questions and answers given in this book have been taken from students and teachers. Some examples are from school textbooks, mainly NCERT books. The answers in these examples are for your reference, only to help you understand how to apply memory techniques to, but we would like to emphasize that you must recheck the answers with your teachers or from your textbooks, as in some books, the answers may differ. In any case, you can make your own memory solution for your answers by following the method taught in each example.

Once these techniques are put into practice, your mind will naturally start functioning the same way. With time, you will start following these without any effort.

We assure you that you will see results in no time and will feel motivated to follow the techniques taught in this book as often as possible. This book will give you an edge over others;

you will have the confidence to face cut-throat competition that is impossible to escape.

Let's get started on an amazing journey of knowledge and explore the eternal potential of your brain.

★★★ HOW IS THIS BOOK DIFFERENT ★★★ FROM THE EARLIER BOOK?

This book purely comprises memorization solutions for academic problems, which will help students memorize their vast syllabus easily and retain it for longer. In this book we have taken more than 300 examples from different school subjects to explain the application of memory techniques directly in these courses, such as memorizing long answers, vocabulary, foreign language words, history dates, the elements of the periodic table, chemical compounds and reactions, science diagrams and terminologies, general knowledge facts and information, multiplication tables, trigonometry, and physics formulas.

Apart from academics, the techniques can be applied to various fields and by people from all walks of life. The application of these memory techniques for all sorts of people has been covered in our previous book, *How to Memorize Anything*, where we have used these techniques for various things, like memorizing shopping lists, card details, names and faces, bank account numbers or passwords, and to-do lists. They are also useful in planning trips or events, taking notes and improving concentration.

PART A

WHAT IS MEMORY?
SOME TECHNIQUES YOU MUST KNOW

CHAPTER 1

★ ★ ★

SMART WORK VS HARD WORK

As a child, you must have heard the famous story of the thirsty crow who dropped pebbles into a pot to get to the water. Now imagine the story set in the twenty-first century: That crow, along with his grandson, is searching for water again. Yet again, they come across a pot with just a little water, and they are not able to drink it. The hard-working grandfather crow starts collecting pebbles one by one, just like he did earlier, and throws them into the pot. The younger one, however, just smiles and flies away—only to bring back a straw! Smart, isn't it?

What we can learn from this story is that there are always two ways to complete a task: hard work or smart work. And the wisest is the one that combines the two to get the best result.

Over the course of time, the amount of information being shared across the globe has increased manifold. Students are getting a lot of information from the Internet, from their peer groups and from school. This is overburdening them to memorize lots of details. This is because in the present education system, they are mainly being tested on their memory. So, in spite of working so hard throughout the year, students struggle to achieve their desired results. Information is learnt by rote, but with time it is forgotten, as there is just too much material out there.

For students, not being able to memorize what they're studying, failing to recall answers during their exams and forgetting crucial information can make it impossible to get high scores. The blame, invariably, falls on memory. Their result makes them believe they have a weak memory and an inability to recall things. However, they couldn't be more wrong in this assumption!

Let's first understand what memory is. Memory is a process by which our brain stores information about the world, to give us a sense of who we are. What is stored in our memory is specific and personal, because we are all unique, but there's one thing common to us all—the immense potential of human memory.

A question that may cross your mind is: if the potential of human memory is common in all human beings, then why are some people brighter and more successful than others?

The answer to this is simple.
The secret is in the *way* successful people use the power of their memory.

It is somewhat similar to the way people use smart phones nowadays. For some, it is about clicking and sharing pictures, chatting or messaging, and social networking. But for others, it is used for more than that. These people run their businesses, track their finances and manage their fitness—all using a single device. Not because their phone is more advanced, but because they know how to use it in the best possible manner and get the most out of it.

Just like we learn to use any gadget or machine, we need to train ourselves to use our brain to access its highest potential. There is no such thing as good memory or bad memory; it's all about *trained* memory or *untrained* memory. And those who know the mantra of optimally utilizing their memory, succeed, while others struggle.

For example, if we ask you to recall the colours of a rainbow, you may not take long. The word VIBGYOR would immediately come to mind, as this is how you were taught to remember this information in early schooling.

But if we ask you to name the excretory organs of the human body, will you be able to answer as quickly? We don't think so.

So, ask yourself this: were you more intelligent when you learnt about rainbows? Is it that by the time you came to study excretory organs, most of your memory was already used up?

No! Both assumptions are incorrect. It's actually only about the *way* you memorized the information.

In the first example, you made use of a memory technique, where each letter of the word VIBGYOR is helping you remember the colours of the rainbow in their correct sequence. This technique of forming a single word using the starting letter of each word to be memorized is called an acronym.

So, had you memorized the names of the excretory organs as SKILL (skin, kidneys, intestine, liver and lungs), you would have remembered them later in your life.

This book will open the door to an amazing world of many such interesting memory techniques, which, if followed and practised regularly, can change your academic performance. The techniques are based on the principles of *association* and *visualization*, through which our brains work. These can make the process of memorization very easy and lots of fun and will help you recall information in a more structured way.

CHAPTER 2

★★★

WHY WE CANNOT CONCENTRATE

Lack of concentration is a common problem almost everyone faces nowadays, especially students. With a number of distractions around us, like TVs, the Internet and mobile phones, it is not surprising. So, what exactly is concentration? Concentration is the skill that is required to do any work with 100 per cent efficiency. It is absolutely essential for any learning to take place.

After just a few minutes of studying, students often complain that they are not able to concentrate and ask for a break. Surprisingly, we find the same set of children spending hours intently watching movies or playing games on their mobile phones with full concentration. So, what is the root of the problem—is it a lack of concentration? Actually, it's a lack of interest. The key to concentration is *interest*.

If you think about it, you will notice that you can easily concentrate on things or tasks you are interested in. Have you ever commanded your mind to concentrate on a movie? Or for that matter, have you had to remind yourself to remember the story so that you can share it with your friends the next day? We're quite sure the answer is never. It's a spontaneous process.

However, you'll notice that in spite of making all efforts to command your mind to concentrate while studying, it keeps wandering, and all sorts of unrelated thoughts start clouding your mind. To understand why this happens, let's introspect. What is it about movies or games that make them interesting enough to engage with, without interruption? Well, both keep us in suspense about what is going to happen next, the colourful moving images or characters keep us glued to our screens, and the music and dialogues fill us with all kinds of emotions. Some people tear up while watching an emotional scene, and some feel scared during horror movies. Why?

Because they feel emotionally connected to the characters. Due to all this, our mind never wanders and stays glued to the movie.

Therefore, we can say: the mind understands the language of images, colours, music and emotions.

But we may not find this level of suspense and emotion in our study material.

So, how do we concentrate here? The key to improve concentration when it comes to academics is to visualize and connect the information that you are learning with images and emotions, because that is the language your mind understands best. If you follow these methods while studying, your text will take the shape of a movie, and you will be totally engrossed in what happens next. If you follow this technique, you will notice that your mind does not wander to unnecessary thoughts and remains focused on the matter at hand.

★★★ SECRET TIP ★★★

IF YOU NEED TO CONCENTRATE, GIVE YOUR MIND THE INFORMATION IN A LANGUAGE IT UNDERSTANDS, I.E., THE LANGUAGE OF IMAGES.

If you visualize the information as a movie or a game, it will help you convert uninteresting and abstract concepts from your school syllabus into a language that your mind can understand. This way, you can make your studies interesting and concentrate well on all your subjects.

★★★

CHAPTER 3

SECRET PRINCIPLES OF MEMORY

Before embarking on the journey of learning memory techniques and methods, let's assess your present memory level through a simple task.

Here is a list of twenty objects. Now, memorize these words in the same sequence. Using a stopwatch, record the time you take to memorize this list of twenty words.

The words are:

- Tiger
- Towel
- Sandalwood
- Roses
- Pencil box
- Angel
- Crayons

- Bucket
- Toothbrush
- Carpet
- Books
- Car
- Door
- Chocolates

- Stars
- Pen
- Lamp
- Table
- Mobile
- Sofa

Time you took to memorize: _____

Although this list consists of simple words, you must have taken ten to fifteen minutes to memorize it in the same sequence, right? And while recollecting, you might have made some mistakes too. Don't be disheartened; after playing the following interesting game, you will soon be able to do the same.

In this, we are going to tell you a few simple words. Imagine these words in your mind and associate them to a story we are going to tell you. Try to visualize it all in *action*, as if it is happening in front of you.

The words are:

- **Mickey Mouse:** The moment you think of Mickey Mouse, an image of the famous Disney character must have appeared in your mind.

- **Car:** Now, visualize Mickey Mouse sitting in a blue car. Can you imagine Mickey Mouse driving a blue car?
- **Toffees:** Visualize the blue car being full of toffees.

- **Pineapple juice:** Imagine that the car runs out of petrol; instead of petrol, it is filled with pineapple juice.

- **Donkey:** Imagine that the car goes full speed after being filled with the pineapple juice, but suddenly a donkey starts crossing the road and blocks the way.
- **Parrot:** Picture the donkey sneezing hard and a parrot coming out of its nose!

- **Moon:** The parrot that flew out of the donkey's nose takes off for the moon.

- **Snow White:** On the moon, Snow White, the princess from the well-known fairy tale, is standing there to welcome the parrot.
- **Popcorn:** Visualize that Snow White is munching on some popcorn.

- **Football:** While eating, one kernel of popcorn falls and gets inflated to form a big football!

- **Spiderman:** The popcorn-football bursts, and the Marvel superhero Spiderman comes out of it.

- **Aeroplane:** Next, picture that Spiderman has entrapped an empty aeroplane in its web.
- **Red carpet:** Inside the aeroplane, a massive red carpet has been rolled out.
- **Black cat:** A black cat is walking on the red carpet.
- **Red Fort:** Now picture that the black cat jumps on to the Red Fort.

OK, let's stop here.

Now, try to recollect all the words you visualized above and write them down in sequential order below:

---------------- ---------------- ----------------

---------------- ---------------- ----------------

---------------- ---------------- ----------------

---------------- ---------------- ----------------

---------------- ---------------- ----------------

If you visualized the above story properly, then you must have been able to recollect the words in the right sequence. If not, go back and read the associations once more and then list the words again. See how you fare; we are sure you will get it right.

Let's move further in the word game.

- **Towel:** Picture the Red Fort covered with many towels.
- **Trophy:** Below each towel, someone has hidden some trophies—some big, some small.
- **School bag:** Visualize that you spot the biggest trophy and find a school bag inside it.
- **Einstein:** From the school bag jumps out Einstein, who starts walking around.
- **Swimming pool:** Einstein spots a swimming pool and decides to take a dip!

Through these exercises you must have understood the process of associating one object with the previous, making a long chain of words. You can really have fun with this method as the scenarios are quite imaginative. Try a few more! Here are some additional words that you can use to make your own chain. Just keep connecting the words to continue the story.

The words are:

- **Dragon**
- **Oranges**
- **Sandwiches**
- **Mirror**
- **Chocolates**
- **Blue shoes**
- **Tent**
- **Bike**
- **Sunglasses**
- **Door**

Now, try to recall all thirty words from the beginning of this exercise while replaying the story in your mind. You can think of this as a movie or a video! This way you will be able to recollect all of them.

So, how did it go? Did you fare better than when you tried the exercise with the first twenty words? Were you able to memorize all thirty words in their sequence? We are sure that this time around you got most of the words right. This is because using this technique doesn't require a lot of effort. It makes the whole process more creative, whereby you memorize while having fun. You must now be wondering how you were able to do it so effortlessly. This is because you unknowingly used the basic principles or laws of memory, which are important for good registration of any information.

The three laws of memory can be summarized in a single word: **AIR**

ASSOCIATION

IMAGINATION

RIDICULOUS THINKING

★★★ AIR: THREE LAWS OF MEMORY ★★★

The first law is the LAW OF ASSOCIATION. According to this, when we connect new information to older information that is already present in the brain, the old information acts like a peg (a nail or a hook) to hold on to the new one, which makes its registration in the brain stronger.

Let's compare the two methods of word registration—the first is the method you used to memorize the first list of twenty words at the beginning of chapter, and the second is what was used for the list of thirty words using association. Now, answer these questions:

- **In which method do you think registration of the word list is faster?**

- **In which case did you recollect words more easily and effortlessly?**

The second method, which uses associations, makes it easier to remember words. In the first case, there is a high chance that you might get confused by your memorized list after a few hours or a day, but with the association method, you will be able to recall the thirty words correctly even after a week or maybe even longer, because you're connecting the words together to make a story. So the retention period is longer when you follow the laws of memory. The law of association works along with the second law, the LAW OF IMAGINATION.

Think of where you are recalling this list from. It is from your imagination, because while associating, you were asked to imagine all these links in your mind. With those images in your mind (which you created yourself) you are able to recall everything so quickly, as our **brain stores information in pictures**.

Had you rote memorized the list, you would have had to repeat the words again and again. However, seeing it clearly in your mind as a story is enough for better registration.

Now, the third law of memory, the LAW OF RIDICULOUS THINKING, which is equally important.

Have you ever filled your car with pineapple juice instead of petrol or diesel? Have you ever seen a parrot coming out of a donkey's nose? Or towels covering the Red Fort? All these associations or images were strange, weird and just ridiculous. That is why you could register them quickly, because our mind registers unusual and ridiculous information faster.

Using this AIR principle, you can memorize anything easily. We will explore some more techniques in the coming chapters that use this principle of AIR.

★ ★ ★

CHAPTER 4

★ ★ ★

CHAIN METHOD:
THE EASIEST WAY TO LEARN

All memory, whether trained or untrained, is based on association, which you learnt about in the previous chapter. If you look back, you will be surprised to discover that you have been using association throughout your life, consciously or subconsciously. Many of you must have been taught the spelling of **'believe'** by remembering the phrase: *Never believe a lie*. Let's analyse this word:

Spelling of 'lie' → **Old information**
Spelling of 'believe' → **New information**

The association between the old and the new information helps us remember.

In the same way, the names of the planets in our solar system were memorized by many of us with the help of the famous sentence: *My Very Educated Mother Just Served Us Noodles*. Here, the first letter of each word is the first letter of each planet in the exact sequence, such as Mercury, Venus and Earth.

The colours of the rainbow were (and still are) remembered through the acronym *VIBGYOR*.

We have been using this law of association to remember many similar things. But the application of this method has been very limited, although it offers vast possibilities. The system of association can be applied to all kinds of information—words, paragraphs, formulas, spellings, numbers, vocabulary and more.

So, if you think and recall the list of thirty words right now (which you memorized in the last chapter), you will be able to do it with ease. Try to answer the following questions:

Who was sitting in the blue car? _
What was filled in the blue car? _
What blocked the way of the car? _ _ _ _ _ _ _ _ _ _ _ _ _ _ _ _ _ _ _
Who was standing on the moon? _

Now mentally revisit the sequence in your mind and write all the words in the same sequence in the spaces given below:

_ _ _ _ _ _ _ _ _ _ _ _ _ _ _ _   _ _ _ _ _ _ _ _ _ _ _ _ _ _ _ _   _ _ _ _ _ _ _ _ _ _ _ _ _ _ _ _
_ _ _ _ _ _ _ _ _ _ _ _ _ _ _ _   _ _ _ _ _ _ _ _ _ _ _ _ _ _ _ _   _ _ _ _ _ _ _ _ _ _ _ _ _ _ _ _
_ _ _ _ _ _ _ _ _ _ _ _ _ _ _ _   _ _ _ _ _ _ _ _ _ _ _ _ _ _ _ _   _ _ _ _ _ _ _ _ _ _ _ _ _ _ _ _
_ _ _ _ _ _ _ _ _ _ _ _ _ _ _ _   _ _ _ _ _ _ _ _ _ _ _ _ _ _ _ _   _ _ _ _ _ _ _ _ _ _ _ _ _ _ _ _
_ _ _ _ _ _ _ _ _ _ _ _ _ _ _ _   _ _ _ _ _ _ _ _ _ _ _ _ _ _ _ _   _ _ _ _ _ _ _ _ _ _ _ _ _ _ _ _
_ _ _ _ _ _ _ _ _ _ _ _ _ _ _ _   _ _ _ _ _ _ _ _ _ _ _ _ _ _ _ _   _ _ _ _ _ _ _ _ _ _ _ _ _ _ _ _
_ _ _ _ _ _ _ _ _ _ _ _ _ _ _ _   _ _ _ _ _ _ _ _ _ _ _ _ _ _ _ _   _ _ _ _ _ _ _ _ _ _ _ _ _ _ _ _
_ _ _ _ _ _ _ _ _ _ _ _ _ _ _ _   _ _ _ _ _ _ _ _ _ _ _ _ _ _ _ _   _ _ _ _ _ _ _ _ _ _ _ _ _ _ _ _
_ _ _ _ _ _ _ _ _ _ _ _ _ _ _ _   _ _ _ _ _ _ _ _ _ _ _ _ _ _ _ _   _ _ _ _ _ _ _ _ _ _ _ _ _ _ _ _
_ _ _ _ _ _ _ _ _ _ _ _ _ _ _ _   _ _ _ _ _ _ _ _ _ _ _ _ _ _ _ _   _ _ _ _ _ _ _ _ _ _ _ _ _ _ _ _

How did you fare? Were you able to recall all the words correctly? We're sure that you must have found it easy to recall these words since you applied *association*.

This method of associating one word with the second, and the second with the third, is called the **Chain Method,** as pieces of information are connected just like loops in a chain. One piece of information leads you to the next if you are associating correctly. This method is highly effective in memorizing long lists of words, answers in point form, points of a speech and more.

Some of you might feel that making an association between two random words is not always easy. But that's not true; you can associate any two unrelated items in more than just one way. Let's try this with two random words—the planet **Jupiter** and the animal **bear**. Many associations can be made between these.

- All bears have emigrated to Jupiter.
- Jupiter is actually a planet of bears.
- You will magically become a bear if you land on Jupiter.
- There are bears swimming in Jupiter's orbit.
- Jupiter is launching bears into space.

Make an association of your own and write it here: _____

_____

_____

_____

Do this activity for any two words of your choice and soon you will get accustomed to the system. It's not only creative but also great fun!

Let's use the Chain Method and practise some more. Here is a list of random objects. Using this method, link the first object to the second, the second to the third, and so on. Visualize it very clearly in your mind, if possible in action and in some ridiculous scenario.

The list is:

- **Badminton racket**
- **Sparrow**
- **Book**
- **Mobile**
- **Fan**
- **Chocolates**
- **Envelope**
- **Tomatoes**
- **Mirror**
- **Spectacles**

Write your associations below. One has been done as an example.

Badminton racket and Chocolates: As I started playing with my badminton racket, chocolates started falling from it.

Chocolates and Sparrow: _____

_____

_____

Sparrow and Envelope: _____

_____

_____

Envelope and Book: _____

_____

_____

Book and Tomatoes: _____

_____

_____

Tomatoes and Mobile: _____
_____
_____

Mobile and Mirror: _____
_____
_____

Mirror and Fan: _____
_____
_____

Fan and Spectacles: _____
_____
_____

HERE'S ANOTHER EXERCISE

Challenge yourself today. Ask your friend or somebody at home to give you a list of fifteen to twenty words, or as many as you feel comfortable with. Surprise them by memorizing these words in sequence, all in the span of a few minutes.

CHAPTER 5

PNN METHOD: NICKNAMES FOR ALL!

In the last chapter, we learnt that it is easier to store information in the form of images. Memorizing words can be difficult, but their images are easily registered in the brain by the association method and imagination. Hence, we can memorize anything by imagining it in pictures and in ridiculous scenarios. However, what about things we don't have an image for, like a difficult or unfamiliar word? Or names of new places or people? What do we do then? For instance, let's look at the following words: *Vietnam, phosphorus, Hungary, glossophobia, cacophony*. These are indeed tough to imagine. To memorize these kinds of words or terminologies, we can use the **Personal Nick Name Method**, or the **PNN Method**. It is called 'personal' as nicknames vary from person to person.

In the movie *3 Idiots*, Aamir Khan played the role of Ranchoddas Shamaldas Chanchad, but his friends called him Rancho. Similarly, we often give nicknames to a person whose name is either long or difficult for us to pronounce. So, in the same way, when we come across a new or difficult word, we should first pronounce it slowly and try to find a word we already know that is similar to this difficult word in terms of pronunciation, or we find an image that is already stored in our personal memory. Then you can use that word as a nickname for the difficult new word.

Let's take the word *Belgium*. If you have never visited Belgium, or have almost no information about this country, you will find it difficult to form an image for the word Belgium in your mind.

However, you can apply the PNN method to memorize this. Let's begin: pronounce Belgium slowly, breaking it into parts like **Bel – gi – um**.

Now, find some familiar words in it, like:

Bell
or
Bell + Gym
or
Bell + Gum

These are just examples. You can come up with any other image; it all depends on your imagination and prior vocabulary.

So you see that through the PNN Method a word like Belgium, which was earlier difficult for you to visualize, is now a clear image for you. You can associate this word with any other information you need to memorize.

The PNN Method is extremely useful and can be used to memorize the following:

- Difficult abstract words
- Technical terms
- Scientific terminologies
- General facts and information
- Names of people and places

We will use this highly efficient method along with other methods in this book to memorize information.

Let's practise some more and understand how to break up abstract words or names into familiar words and images.

S.No.	Abstract words	PNN	Association
1.	Vietnam	Wait + Name	You must **wait** until your **name** is called.
2.	Phosphorus	Fox + for + us	This **fox** is **for us**.
3.	Hungary	Hungry	I'm feeling **hungry**.
4.	Glossophobia	Gloss + phobia	That person has a **phobia** of lip **gloss**.
5.	Cacophony	Cock + phone	A **cock** is talking on the **phone**.

It is important to know that it is not necessary to always associate a word with a familiar rhyming word; any other prior association with or knowledge about that word can also serve as a nickname for it. For instance, Switzerland can be broken into *sweets + land*, but one can also be reminded of watches, which the country is famous for. So, *watch* can be a PNN for the word Switzerland. Similarly, Bharatiya Janata Party may remind someone of an image of a *lotus,* which is the party symbol, while someone else may relate it to Prime Minister *Narendra Modi*. In the same way, Amritsar could remind someone of the Golden Temple. Therefore, the PNN or nickname association differs from person to person.

In short, you can apply PNNs to convert any abstract, intangible or difficult word into a picture and then associate the related information with them easily.

CHAPTER 6

★ ★ ★

RHYME METHOD: LEARNING THE PROPERTIES OF METALS

Memory techniques can be applied to all subjects in the school curriculum, even science! You didn't imagine that, right? It's true! To remember many things, we can apply the various methods that exist, such as the one we will learn about in this chapter—the **Rhyme Method**. To understand how this method works, we have picked a chemistry chapter that discusses the properties of metals, to make the learning easier to relate to.

Let's start by looking at some important physical properties of metals:

1. Metals are malleable—that is, metals can be beaten into thin sheets with a hammer and will not break.
2. Metals are ductile—that is, metals can be drawn or stretched into thin wires.
3. Metals are good conductors of electricity.
4. Metals are good conductors of heat.
5. Metals are lustrous (shiny) and can be polished.
6. Metals are generally hard (except sodium and potassium, which are soft metals).
7. Metals are strong (except sodium and potassium, which are not strong).

8. Metals are solids at room temperature (except mercury, which is a liquid metal).

9. Metals have high melting and boiling points, except sodium and potassium, which have low melting and boiling points.

10. Metals have high densities, except sodium and potassium, which have low densities.

11. Metals are sonorous—that is, metals make a sound when hit with an object.

12. Metals are usually silver or grey in colour, except copper and gold.

(Source: *Science for 9th Class, Part 2* by Lakhmir Singh and Manjit Kaur)

You can memorize the above using a very simple technique called the Rhyme Method. In this method, we associate numbers with images of things that rhyme with it. These images serve as pegs (or hooks) to associate new information with them in order to secure it in your brain. That is why it is also called the Peg Method. This method allows you to remember not only the items in their correct order but also the item's exact position in the list. Isn't that great?

So let's look at a chart of images that we can assign to the numbers one to twelve according to their *rhyming sounds*:

1		2	
ONE	SUN	TWO	SHOE
3		4	
THREE	TREE	FOUR	DOOR

5		6	
FIVE	HIVE	SIX	STICKS
7		8	
SEVEN	LEMON	EIGHT	PLATE
9		10	
NINE	LINE	TEN	HEN
11		12	
ELEVEN	HEAVEN	TWELVE	SHELF

We can extend the number chart for numbers beyond twelve as well; for more details, you can refer to our book *How to Memorize Anything*.

You may choose rhyming items for each number as per your liking. For example, number **one** can be visualized as *sun*, *bun* or *nun* but not as *fun*, as visualizing fun is a bit difficult compared to the rest. Try to visualize clear images instead of abstract ones.

Now, let's use the above rhyme codes to memorize the properties of metals:

★★★ PHYSICAL PROPERTIES OF METALS ★★★

	Rhyme codes	Properties	PNN	Visualization
1.	Sun	Malleable	Mall	There is a special mall on the Sun, where thin sheets of metals are sold.
2.	Shoe	Ductile	Duck	The duck is wearing shoes made of metal pipes.
3.	Tree	Good conductor of electricity	Electric wire	Electric wires are passing through a tree.
4.	Door	Good conductor of heat	Bus conductor + heat	The bus conductor standing at the door is radiating heat.
5.	Hive	Lustrous (shiny)	Shine	The hive in your friend's garden shines even at night.
6.	Sticks	Hard	Hard	Sticks are too hard to break.
7.	Lemon	Strong	Strong	Eating a lemon makes you very strong.
8.	Plate	Solid at room temperature	Solid	This is a very solid plate.

	Rhyme codes	Properties	PNN	Visualization
9.	*Line*	High melting and boiling points	*Boil/Melt*	Seeing the kids standing in a line on a hot summer day made the parents' blood boil and the teachers' hearts melt.
10.	*Hen*	High densities	*Thick and dense*	The hen at the farm has thick and dense muscles.
11.	*Heaven*	Sonorous	*Sound*	In heaven, many melodious sounds can be heard.
12.	*Shelf*	Usually silver/grey in colour	*Silver*	This shelf is made of silver.

You will realize that if you follow the Rhyme Method of memorizing information, it will stay with you for longer, as assigning images makes it easier to recall information.

This method is particularly useful in memorizing information like:

- **Any list consisting of up to twenty items in a sequence.**
- **Long answers in point form.**
- **Points in a speech.**
- **Items whose position numbers are important.**

CHAPTER 7

★★★

SHAPE METHOD: LEARN THE NAMES OF THE LONGEST RIVERS IN THE WORLD

Students are often required to memorize information in a particular sequence. This becomes a little tricky for them, as even a slight change in the order affects the entire result. Let's learn a wonderful method that will help you memorize any information in its correct sequence.

The following are the ten longest rivers in the world:

1. **Nile**
2. **Amazon**
3. **Yangtze**
4. **Mississippi**
5. **Yenisei**
6. **Yellow River**
7. **Ob**
8. **Parana**
9. **Congo**
10. **Amur**

We can memorize the above list by using the peg method for numbers, known as the **Number Shape Method**.

★★★ NUMBER SHAPE METHOD ★★★

In this method, we associate each number (starting from 1) with an image that resembles its shape, so that we can recall that number easily.

Look at the following table:

1 ONE	CANDLE	2 TWO	DUCK
3 THREE	HEART	4 FOUR	CHAIR
5 FIVE	HOOK	6 SIX	HOCKEY STICK
7 SEVEN	AXE	8 EIGHT	SNOWMAN
9 NINE	BALLOON	10 TEN	BAT + BALL

In the chart, you can see that the image associated with its respective number resembles that number very closely. For instance, the candle looks like the number 1, and the number 2 has a curve like the neck of a duck.

Now apply this new method to memorize the longest rivers in the world. To understand this better, let's look at the example below:

The ninth longest river is the Congo.

Congo : Conga drums (*PNN Method*)
9th : Balloons (*Shape Method*)

Visualization: My parents gave me *conga drums* as a birthday gift, which had **balloons** tied to them.

We hope you found the method easy to follow. Let's use the Shape Method along with the PNN Method to memorize the ten longest rivers in the world.

Number	Image	Name of the River	PNN	Visualization
1.	Candle	Nile	Mile	The **candle** is a *mile* long.
2.	Duck	Amazon	Amazon (online shopping site)	The website *Amazon* has exclusive deals on **duck**s.
3.	Heart	Yangtze	Young	One should always be *young* at **heart**.
4.	Chair	Mississippi	Miss is sipping	*Miss is sipping* tea while sitting on a **chair**.
5.	Hook	Yenisei	Yen (currency)	In Japan, you can purchase a silver **hook** for only one *yen*.
6.	Hockey stick	Yellow River	Yellow river	My **hockey stick** fell in the *river*, and now it's *yellow*.
7.	Axe	Ob	O! Baby!	The mother saw her baby reaching for an axe. She screamed, '*O! Baby!* Don't touch that **axe** or you will get hurt.'
8.	Snowman	Parana	Purr	This **snowman** I made *purr*s like a cat.

9.	Balloon	Congo	Conga drums	My parents gave me *conga drums* as a birthday gift, which had **balloon**s tied to them.
10.	Bat + Ball	Amur	Amul (butter)	The kids are playing with **bat**s and a **ball** made of *Amul* butter.

You can see that by using our imagination, we can easily remember any information in sequence by using shapes associated with the numbers.

You can recall the information in whichever way asked.

For example, if we ask you what number the Yellow River is in the list, you can easily remember that the **hockey stick** fell in the *river*, which made it *yellow*; the hockey stick symbolizes the number **6**. Or if we ask you what the eighth longest river is, then **8** reminds you of a **snowman** that *purrs*, which reminds you that the river is the Parana.

In the same way, you can remember lists of prime ministers, Presidents or any other information you are required to know by number or hierarchical position.

CHAPTER 8

HIDE AND SEEK METHOD

Hide-and-seek is a game that all of us have enjoyed playing in our childhood—a fun game in which we used to hide somewhere while the seeker tried to find us. We can play this game to memorize our answers and make our studies interesting and fun too!

However, there is a twist. We will play this game *mentally*, by hiding the information to be memorized in well-known places in our mind and then seeking them using our imagination. Let's understand this with the following question:

Q: What are the conditions affecting the climate of a place?

A: The following are the conditions that influence the climate of a place:

1. Forest area
2. Types of soil
3. Direction of winds
4. Clouds
5. Mountains in that area
6. Built-up area
7. Water bodies in that area
8. Distance from the sea
9. Types of industries in that area

To memorize this answer, we need to choose any **familiar location**, like our classroom, and identify **some points** in the room, **in a sequence**. These points can be, for example:

1. **Door**
2. **Bookshelf**
3. **Speaker**
4. **Blackboard**
5. **Chart**
6. **Teacher's table**
7. **Dustbin**
8. **Windows**
9. **Students**

These nine points now become our 'hiding places' that we need to use to memorize the required information.

To start, we associate the first point of our answer with the first hiding place in our classroom; so, we will associate **forest area** with the **door**. It's like hiding that information in that place in your imagination. So, we proceed this way, and while progressing along the route of the classroom, we continue to place or *hide* each point of our answer one by one. We are making an association between the points of our answer and the respective hiding places in our imagination, all in the correct sequence. It's quite simple and a good way to have fun while you learn.

Now let's look at the answer again and the words or items of association. The following associations can be made to memorize the above answer:

1. **Forest area – Door**
   Visualize that there is a dense *forest* outside the *door*.
2. **Types of soil – Bookshelf**
   On the various shelves of the *bookshelf*, different *types of soil* (black soil, yellow soil, red soil, brown soil, etc.) are displayed.
3. **Direction of winds – Speaker**
   From all *directions*, the *wind* is blowing and going into the *speaker*.
4. **Clouds – Blackboard**
   Imagine *clouds* are coming out of the *blackboard*.
5. **Mountains in that area – Chart**
   Visualize drawings of big *mountains* on the *chart*.
6. **Build-up area – Teacher's table**
   There are models of *buildings* (PNN for build-up area) on the *teacher's table*.
7. **Water bodies in that area – Dustbin**
   The *dustbin* is full of *water bottles* (PNN for water bodies).
8. **Distance from the sea – Windows**
   You look out of the *windows* to know the *distance of the sea* from the classroom.
9. **Types of industries in that area – Students**
   Each *student* is studying different *types of industries* according to their interest.

So while recollecting the answer, you just need to take a mental tour of the hiding places located in the classroom in the same sequence you hid the information. The moment you visualize the hiding place, you will be reminded of the information that you had placed there, like the **door** will remind us of the **forest area**.

This is a famous memory technique and is known by different names—**Loci Method, Journey Method, Placement Method, Memory Palace Method** and **Roman Room Method,** among others.

This memory method is quite useful and can also be used to memorize the following things:

- Points of speeches
- Any list of information in sequence, like checklists or shopping lists
- Long sequences of numbers
- Long answers

So apply this method and ace your subjects.

> THE LOCATION YOU ARE HIDING THE INFORMATION IN SHOULD BE A FAMILIAR PLACE; OTHERWISE, YOU WILL HAVE TO MEMORIZE THE LOCATION TOO. SOME GOOD AND EASY LOCATIONS ARE YOUR OWN ROOM, YOUR HOUSE, OR EVEN A FAMILIAR ROUTE, SUCH AS THE ROUTE YOU TAKE TO TRAVEL TO SCHOOL OR TO A FRIEND'S OR RELATIVE'S HOUSE. SOME AMOUNT OF FAMILIARITY WITH THE LOCATION IS NEEDED FOR THIS METHOD TO WORK SUCCESSFULLY.

Now, if you have to memorize a list of, say, twenty, thirty or even more words or items, then you can either find more places in the same room or use three or more rooms in the house or familiar place to create a list of thirty or more hiding places. Try and see if you're able to apply and use this method effectively. We are sure long, boring answers can be made a lot more interesting and easier by this method.

CHAPTER 9

PHONETIC PEG SYSTEM: LET'S CRACK THE NUMBERS

As students, we need to memorize lot of numerical data, like historical dates, the periodic table, melting/boiling points, the mass of electrons and neutrons, various constants, maths tables, valances and formulas.

Most students lose marks because they find memorizing numerical data difficult. They try to rote memorize all these numbers but tend to get confused in exams, as numbers are abstract. For example, it is very likely that a student whose board exam role number is 8218735 can get confused and write it as 8218357. That's why you are asked to copy it from your hall ticket. Sadly, you will not be allowed to copy any other information asked in exams, including numbers!

But now we know that our mind understands the language of pictures, not numbers. We have learnt the Rhyme Method and the Shape Method to convert numbers into images. However, these methods have their limitations. Hence, we need to make our own language that can convert all kinds of large numbers into pictures. For that we are going to learn an advanced peg method called the **Phonetic Peg Method**.

As the name suggests, according to the phonetic sound of the number, we assign a letter to each digit from 0 to 9. These are summarized in the table below:

NUMBER	CODE
0	s or z
1	t or d
2	n
3	m
4	r
5	l
6	j, ch, sh or g (as in sage)
7	k or ga (as in gun)
8	f or v
9	p or b

Important things to remember while using this method:

- The five vowels—*a, e, i, o, u*—and the soft consonant sounds *wa, ha* and *ya* are not assigned to any number.
- With some of the numbers, there is more than one letter given, but the phonetic sound of these letters is the same in each case. The lips, tongue and teeth are used in the same way to sound 'p' and 'b', 'f' and 'v', 's' and 'z', or 'j', 'sh' and 'ch'.

Let's begin. The following hints can help you memorize the above codes easily, so let's look at these:

O – The sun is round like a zero, and the first letter of 'sun' is 's'. Similarly, the first letter in 'zero' is 'z'.

1 – A small 't' or 'd' has one down stroke.

2 – A small 'n' requires two down strokes.

3 – A small 'm' requires three down strokes, or the shape of 'm' is similar to 3.

4 – The pronunciation of 'four' in many languages ends in 'r'. In Hindi it's *char*, in Latin it's *quattuor* and in Spanish it's *cuatro*.

5 – In Roman numerals, 'L' means 50; here, a small 'l' means five.

6 – The mirror image of 6 is similar to 'j'. It can also be represented by the sounds 'ch', 'sh' or 'g'.

7 – Two inverted sevens can form a 'k'.

8 – The shape of the small 'f' in cursive writing is like 8.

9 – 'p' is the mirror image of 9, while 'b' can be turned around to look like 9.

To master numbers, you need to practise and remember this table. Embed it in your brain. Remember, it took you days to master alphabets in your childhood, so spend a little time getting this number-phonic system memorized, and believe us, you will not regret it. With a little practice and the clues given to remember them, you can master them easily.

Exercise your brain by filling in the blanks in the table given below. If you are unable to recall the corresponding number or sound, go back and review the hints given after the phonetic table above:

2 = _____	b = _____	l = _____	3 = _____
k = _____	5 = _____	4 = _____	n = _____

t = _____	r = _____	9 = _____	f = _____
_____	_____	_____	_____
j = _____	8 = _____	p = _____	7 = _____
_____	_____	_____	_____
s = _____	2 = _____	6 = _____	0 = _____
_____	_____	_____	_____
m = _____	g = _____	t = _____	1 = _____
_____	_____	_____	_____

★★★ CREATING WORDS FROM NUMBERS ★★★

Now it's time to use the above codes. With this, you can translate any number into letters and can form a word, which can then be converted into an image for visualization.

Example 1:

$$47$$
$$4 = r \quad 7 = k$$
$$47 = r + k$$

Just think of some word that has the sound of 'r' and 'k' in it.
47 = r + k = **RacK**

RacK is one of the possible words; you may think of some other words, like RocK.

★★★ SECRET TIP ★★★

WHILE CONVERTING NUMBERS INTO WORDS, WE CAN
ADD ANY VOWEL (A, E, I, O, U) OR ANY OTHER LETTERS
IN BETWEEN THE FIXED CODES THAT DO NOT REPRESENT
ANY NUMBER IN THE ABOVE PHONETIC CODES TABLE.
WHEN TWO OR MORE WORDS COME TO YOUR MIND FOR
A PARTICULAR NUMBER, CHOOSE THE WORD YOU CAN
SEE CLEARLY IN YOUR MIND.

Example 2:

94

9 = p or b   4 = r

As 9 has two letters according to the phonetic system, we can use
either one of them and convert it into some word accordingly.

94 = b + r

94 = BeaR

Some other possible words: BaR, BoRe, BeeR, BoaR, BooR.

94 = p + r

Some possible words: PeaR, PuRe, PooR, PoRe.

See, this method is easy. All you need to know is the table
and it'll be very easy to master. Using the above method, you can
convert any number into words or images. These images will
serve as pegs to associate information with them.

PHONETICS: SOUND IS MORE IMPORTANT THAN SPELLING

In the phonetic peg system, it is important that you pay attention only to the *sound* or *pronunciation* of words and not to the spelling.

1. In words like **cone** and **coal**, the sound of *c* is like *k*, so we shall treat it like *k*—**coal** will be converted to **75** (koal).
2. Similarly, **doll** will not be converted into 155 but into '15, as we hear only one *l*, so we shall consider only one *l* instead of two.
3. In **knife**, we shall not consider *k*, since it is silent. Similarly, in **fork** we shall not consider *r*, as it is silent. So **fork** will be **87**, not 847.
4. The word **accent** will be pronounced 'aksent'. So, the letters *k*, *s, n* and *t* would correspond to the number **7021**, not to 7721.
5. **Sage** will be converted to **06**, not to 07. In the pronunciation of sage, 'g' has sounds like 'j', which represents 6. But in words like **kangaroo**, 'g' has the soft sound of 'ga', which represents **7** in phonetics.

HOW DOES THE PHONETIC SYSTEM HELP AVOID CONFUSION?

Let's memorize 8218735—the role number we discussed earlier—using the Phonetic Peg Method:

8	2	1	8	7	3	5
f	n	d	f	k	m	l
fond of kamal						

Now in the exam hall, when the student tries to decode 'fond of kamal', it can be decoded as **8218735**.

FØND ØF KÅMÅL
↓ ↓ ↓   ↓ ↓ ↓ ↓
8 2 1   8 7 3 5

Let's practise some more! Let's code the following number—8218357.

8	2	1	8	3	5	7
f	n	d	f	m	l	k
fond of milk						

As you can see 'fond of milk' is a completely different image from 'fond of kamal'. A student could get confused between 735 and 357, but they won't get confused between 'kamal' and 'milk', as we have distinct images of the two. Isn't that great? You can practise this with other numerals and see the results!

Hence, you can see that the Phonetic Peg Method helps us convert meaningless, abstract numbers into meaningful images, which can be easily memorized. This reduces the need for rote memorizing and eliminates confusion. It reduces the burden on the brain.

Here is a chart of some possible codes for 00 to 99 using phonetic pegs. These codes are given for your reference; you can also make your own codes by following the rules given above to make words from numbers.

00	SauSe	25	NaiL	50	LaSe	75	KoaL (coal)
01	SuiT	26	NaCHo (snack)	51	LuDo	76	KaSH (cash)
02	SuN	27	NecK	52	LioN	77	KaKe (cake)
03	SuMo (wrestler)	28	NiFe (knife)	53	LiMe	78	KoFee (coffee)
04	SiR (teacher)	29	NiPpo	54	LaRa (Brian)	79	KaP (cap)
05	SaLe	30	MesS	55	LiLy	80	FuSe
06	SaGe	31	MaT	56	LeeCH	81	FeeT
07	SKy	32	MooN	57	LaKe	82	FaN
08	SoFa	33	MaM	58	LeaF	83	F.M. (radio)
09	SoaP	34	aMiR	59	LaB	84	FiRe
10	DoSa	35	MaiL	60	JuiSe	85	FiLe
11	DaD	36	MatCH (stick)	61	JeT	86	FiSH
12	DeN	37	MiKe	62	JeaN(s)	87	FoK (fork)
13	DaM	38	M.F. (Husain)	63	JaM	88	FiFa
14	DR (doctor)	39	MaP	64	JaR	89	F.P. (fountain pen)
15	DoL (doll)	40	RoSe	65	JaiL	90	BuS
16	DiSH	41	RaT	66	JudGe	91	BaT
17	DecK	42	RaiN	67	JacKy (Jackie Chan)	92	BuN

18	DwarF	43	RaM	68	J.F. (jelly fish)	93	BoM (bomb)
19	TaP	44	ReaR	69	JeeP	94	BeaR
20	NoSe	45	RaiL	70	KisS	95	BelL
21	NeT	46	RiDGe	71	KiTe	96	BuSH
22	NuN	47	RacK	72	KoNe (cone)	97	BiKe
23	NeeM	48	RooF	73	KoMb (comb)	98	B.F. (best friend)
24	NehRu (Jawaharlal Nehru)	49	RoPe	74	KaR (car)	99	Baby

You might think it is very difficult to convert numbers into such codes, but from our experience of teaching thousands of students in our workshops, we can assure you that once you are comfortable with the sounds of the numbers, the rest can be learnt in a matter of two days. To lock in the sounds of the numbers in your memory, you have to start practising right from this moment.

Now practise by completing the following table:

Trouble = _____	820 = _____
Designer = _____ (g is silent)	171 = _____
Karishma = _____	140 = _____
Numbers = _____	395 = _____
Raipur = _____	5071 = _____
Eraser = _____	32014 = _____

★★★ ANSWERS ★★★

Trouble =	1495
Designer = (g is silent)	1024
Karishma =	7463
Numbers =	23940
Raipur =	494
Eraser =	404

820 =	fins
171 =	ticket
140 =	tears
395 =	mobile
5071 =	loose kit
32014 =	monster

★★★

PART B

ACE THE SCHOOL SYLLABUS: APPLICATION OF MEMORY TECHNIQUES

I. GENERAL KNOWLEDGE

CHAPTER 10

COUNTRIES AND THEIR CAPITALS

Knowledge about the world is vast, and the more we know about it, the more we want to learn about it. But the problem is not gaining knowledge; it is retaining it. Students, no matter what class they are in or level they are at, are required to acquire information; however, they often tend to get confused when it comes to memorizing and recalling it.

Using the PNN Method can make it easier for students, as they can easily memorize information, such as countries and their respective capitals, by visualizing it through humorous associations. Let's look at some examples. We start with the word **Belgium**, which we learnt earlier.

Example 1:

Country	:	**Belgium**
PNN	:	Bell + gym
Capital	:	**Brussels**
PNN	:	Brush

Visualization: *You are cleaning a **bell** in the **gym** with your big tooth**brush**.*

Example 2:

Country	:	**Russia**
PNN	:	Rush
Capital	:	**Moscow**
PNN	:	Mosque

Visualization: *The person is late for prayers and is **rush**ing towards the **mosque**.*

Example 3:

Country	:	**Egypt**
PNN	:	Pyramid
Capital	:	**Cairo**
PNN	:	Car

Visualization: *You are driving around the **pyramid** in your **car**.*

	COUNTRIES and CAPITALS	PNN	VISUALIZATION
1.	Canada Ottawa	Can Tower	The huge **tower** is made of **cans**.
2.	Chile Santiago	Chilli Saint + go	The **saint** is **go**ing to eat only **chillies** today.
3.	Cuba Havana	Cube Heaven	Everyone in **heaven** is busy playing with a Rubik's **cube**.
4.	Denmark Copenhagen	Den + mark Coupon for (water) gun	The person is getting a **coupon** for a water **gun** to **mark** his **den** in the adventure game.
5.	Dominica Roseau	Domino's Pizza Rose	You are being served a pizza with **rose** toppings at **Domino's**.
6.	Haiti Port-au-Prince	Hat Port for a prince	That is a **port for a prince** who wears large **hats**.
7.	Hungary Budapest	Hungry Buddha + paste	The **Buddha** is distributing **paste** to **hungry** people.

8.	Poland Warsaw	Pole War + saw	You **saw** a **war** while sitting on a **pole**.
9.	Switzerland Bern	Sweets Burn	You start making a batch of **sweets**, but it **burns**.
10.	Vietnam Hanoi	Wait + name Hen	The **hen** is **wait**ing for her **name** to be announced.

We are sure you found this method more interesting than rote memorization! To master this skill, try making your own association for the following countries and their capitals:

	COUNTRIES and CAPITALS	PNN	VISUALIZATION
1.	Bolivia La Paz	Ball Pass	
2.	Oman Muscat		
3.	Morocco Rabat		
4.	Jordan Amman		
5.	Germany Berlin		
6.	Ecuador Quito		

7.	Bahrain Manama		
8.	Cameroon Yaounde		
9.	Fiji Suva		
10.	Indonesia Jakarta		

CHAPTER II

★ ★ ★

BOOKS AND AUTHORS

In school as well as in competitive exams, we are often asked to name authors and the books written by them. And many times, most of us find it difficult to recall things when we need to, as there are many books we have learnt about.

However, if we use memory techniques, it's not that difficult. Using the PNN Method, we can easily memorize book names along with their respective authors by visualizing them through hilarious associations. Let's look at some examples:

Example 1:

Book Name : *The History of Tom Jones, a Foundling*

PNN : Tom and Jerry (the cartoon series)

Author : Henry Fielding

PNN : hen + fielding

Visualization : *In my history book, I found **Tom and Jerry** batting on the pitch and a **hen fielding**.*

Example 2:

Book Name	:	*The Monk Who Sold His Ferrari*
PNN	:	monk + sell + Ferrari
Author	:	Robin Sharma
PNN	:	robin (bird)
Visualization	:	A **monk** is **sell**ing his **Ferrari** to a **robin**.

Now, let's look at this table, which has more books and their authors.

	Books and Authors	PNN	Visualization
1.	*Grandma's Bag of Stories* Sudha Murty	grandma's bag Sudha's + Maruti	**Grandma's bag** is in **Sudha's Maruti**.
2.	*How to Win Friends and Influence People* Dale Carnegie	win friends Dale + car + Maggi	**Dale** is driving a **car** while eating **Maggi** in order to **win** more **friends**.
3.	*The Secret* Rhonda Byrne	secret Honda + brain	The **secret** to driving a **Honda** is in your **brain**.

	Books and Authors	PNN	Visualization
4.	*The Alchemist* Paulo Coelho	all chemist Polo + coal	**All chemist**s eat the mint **Polo** to get rid of the smell of **coal**.
5.	*The Adventures of Sherlock Holmes* Arthur Conan Doyle	share + locked + homes earth + corner + doll	Please **share** the addresses of the **locked homes**, as in one of the **corners** of the **earth** is a **doll** who needs a home.
6.	*Oliver Twist* Charles Dickens	liver + twist Charlie + chickens	Your **liver** will get **twist**ed if you eat **Charlie**'s **chickens**.
7.	*Five on a Treasure Island* Enid Blyton	treasure + island need + fly + ton	To find the **treasure** on the **island** you **need** to catch a **ton** of **flies**.
8.	*The Hobbit* J.R.R. Tolkien	habit jar + token	As a **habit**, I always keep a **jar** of **token**s.
9.	*The Diary of a Young Girl* Anne Frank	diary + young girl Anne + frank	In her **diary** as a **young girl**, **Anne**'s notes were very **frank**.
10.	*Alice's Adventures in Wonderland* Lewis Carroll	lice (insects) + wonderland singing carols	The **lice** in **wonderland** are **singing carols**.
11.	*Wings of Fire* A.P.J. Abdul Kalam	wings + fire Abdul Kalam	President **Abdul Kalam** invented special **wings** that were made of **fire**.

	Books and Authors	PNN	Visualization
12.	*The Old Man and the Sea* Ernest Hemingway	old man + sea nest + hummingbird + away	The **old man** sitting by the **sea** saw the **nest** of a **hummingbird** far **away**.
13.	*The Blue Umbrella* Ruskin Bond	blue umbrella rusk (biscuit) + in + pond	You used your **blue umbrella** to save the **rusk** from falling **in**to the **pond**.
14.	*The Fountainhead* Ayn Rand	fountain + head iron + sand	The **fountain**'s **head** is made of **iron**, and when it is turned on, **sand** comes out of it instead of water.
15.	*Pride and Prejudice* Jane Austen	bride + jaundice jail + ten	The **bride** had **jaundice** but was still sent to **jail** for **ten** days.

★★★ **PRACTICE TIME** ★★★

Now practise and memorize the following books and their authors using the above memory techniques:

	Books and Authors	PNN	Visualization
1.	*A Tale of Two Cities* Charles Dickens		
2.	*Madhushala* Harivansh Rai Bachchan		
3.	The Man in the Brown Suit Agatha Christie		
4.	*The Room on the Roof* Ruskin Bond		
5.	*The 7 Habits of Highly Effective People* Stephen Covey		

CHAPTER 12

INVENTIONS AND INVENTORS

Questions about various inventions, discoveries and their inventors are being asked in many competitive exams. By using the PNN and Phonetic Methods, you can memorize the names of inventors along with the year in which a particular invention was made.

Invention	Inventor
Electromagnetic waves	Heinrich Rudolf Hertz
Air conditioning (in 1902)	Willis Carrier
Google (in 1998)	Sergey Brin and Larry Page
Mobile phone (in 1973)	Martin Cooper
Ceiling fan (in 1882)	Philip Diehl
Radio (in 1895)	Guglielmo Marconi
Video game (in 1967)	Ralph Baer
Penicillin (in 1928)	Alexander Fleming
Medical thermometer (in 1866)	Thomas Allbutt
Sewing machine (in 1846)	Elias Howe

Note: The information above has been referenced from https://www.examsbook.com/list-of-inventions-and-inventors-gk-questionsquestions/1

We will memorize the above details by making PNNs for the names of these inventors and their inventions, wherever required, and by visualizing the association between the two. The year of inventions, wherever given, can be further added by converting them into images using the Phonetic Method.

1. **Electromagnetic waves – Heinrich Rudolf Hertz**

Electromagnetic waves	:	Electromagnet (*PNN Method*)
Heinrich Rudolf Hertz	:	Hen + rich + rude + wolf + heart (*PNN Method*)
Visualization	:	The **rich hen** attracted the **rude wolf**'s **heart** using her **electromagnet**.

2. **Air conditioning – Willis Carrier in 1902**

Air Conditioning	:	AC (*PNN Method*)
Willis Carrier	:	Will + carrier (*PNN Method*)
1902	:	sun (*Phonetic Method*)
Visualization	:	You're telling your friend that if he wants to purchase an **AC**, then one from the company **Carrier will** be good as it beats the *sun*'s heat.

3. **Google – Sergey Brin and Larry Page in 1998**

Sergey Brin	:	Surgery of brain (*PNN Method*)
Larry Page	:	Lorry (*PNN Method*)
1998	:	B.F. (best friend) (*Phonetic Method*)
Visualization	:	Due to an emergency, the doctor performed **surgery** on my *best friend*'s **brain** in a **lorry**, and I updated his status on his **Google** account.

4. **Mobile Phone – Martin Cooper in 1973**

Martin Cooper	:	Market + tin + copper (*PNN Method*)

| 1973 | : | Komb (comb - *Phonetic Method*) |
| Visualization | : | A new **mobile phone** made of **tin** and **copper**, and that can be used as a *comb* is launched in the **market**. |

5. **Ceiling Fan – Philip Diehl in 1882**

Philip Diehl	:	Philips + Delhi (*PNN Method*)
1882	:	green* (*colour code for this century*)
18**82**	:	fan (*Phonetic Method*)
Visualization	:	The electronics company **Philips** is launching its special range of *green* **ceiling** *fans* in **Delhi**.

6. **Radio – Guglielmo Marconi in 1895**

Guglielmo Marconi	:	macaroni (*PNN Method*)
1895	:	green* + bell (*Phonetic Method*)
Visualization	:	After preparing **macaroni** by following a recipe on a **radio** show, the mother rang a *green bell* to call her children for dinner.

7. **Video Games – Ralph Baer in 1967**

Ralph Baer	:	Rough bear (*PNN Method*)
1967	:	Jackie (*Phonetic Method*)
Visualization	:	A **rough**-looking **bear** is playing **video games** with *Jackie* Chan.

8. **Penicillin – Alexander Fleming in 1928**

Penicillin	:	Pen + silly (*PNN Method*)
Alexander Fleming	:	Alexander + flame (*PNN Method*)
1928	:	knife (*Phonetic Method*)

---

* You can refer to page 121 of Chapter 21 for the colours of the centuries.

| Visualization | : | **Alexander** is giving his friends a **silly pen** with a **flame**, instead of a *knife*, to cut vegetables. |

9. Medical Thermometer – Thomas Allbutt in 1866

Thomas Allbutt	:	Thermos + all birds (*PNN Method*)
1866	:	green* + judge (*Phonetic Method*)
Visualization	:	**All** the **birds** are carrying a *green* **thermos** in their beaks, and a *judge* is checking their temperatures with a **thermometer**.

10. Sewing Machine – Elias Howe in 1846

Elias Howe	:	Lice (insect) + hive (*PNN Method*)
1846	:	green* + rag (*Phonetic Method*)
Visualization	:	The **lice** in the **hive** are stitching a *green rag* using a **sewing machine**.

Don't restrict these methods to just these ten examples; explore more inventions and discoveries and memorize them using the memory techniques to update your knowledge about the various inventions we use every day.

CHAPTER 13

PRESIDENTS OF INDIA

As you will recall, we memorized the ten longest rivers in the world using the Shape Method in one of the earlier chapters. The Shape Method is particularly useful when things are to be memorized in a specific sequence. For example, if somebody asks you to name the fifth President of India, you need to know not just the name of the President but also their position in the sequence. So let's learn how to memorize the list of Presidents of India in its right order:

1. Dr Rajendra Prasad
2. Dr Sarvepalli Radhakrishnan
3. Zakir Husain
4. Varahagiri Venkata Giri
5. Fakhruddin Ali Ahmed
6. Neelam Sanjiva Reddy
7. Giani Zail Singh
8. Ramaswamy Venkataraman
9. Dr Shankar Dayal Sharma
10. Kocheril Raman Narayanan
11. Dr A.P.J. Abdul Kalam
12. Pratibha Patil
13. Pranab Mukherjee
14. Ram Nath Kovind

Earlier we associated the numbers from one to ten with shapes that were similar to the numerals. In the same way, we can memorize the list by using the Shape Method; however, we need a few more images here, as we have numbers greater than ten. Let's extend the shape method chart for the numbers eleven to twenty (as shown below) and use the chart in the earlier chapter for the numbers up to ten.

11 ELEVEN	 ROAD	12 TWELVE	 CAP
13 THIRTEEN	 BUTTERFLY	14 FOURTEEN	 BOAT
15 FIFTEEN	 SITAR	16 SIXTEEN	 ELEPHANT TRUNK
17 SEVENTEEN	 SANDWICH	18 EIGHTEEN	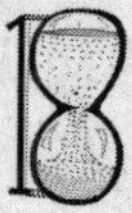 HOURGLASS
19 NINETEEN	 COMPASS	20 TWENTY	 SNAKE

Let's now use the Shape Method along with the PNN Method to memorize the list of Indian Presidents in order as follows:

	Picture of number	Name of the President	PNN	Visualization
1.	Candle	Rajendra Prasad	Raja (name of a boy) + present (gift)	Your friend **Raja present**s a *candle* to you on your birthday.
2.	Duck	Sarvepalli Radhakrishnan	serve + Radha and Krishna	In that restaurant, *duck*s **serve** food to **Radha** and **Krishna**.
3.	Heart	Zakir Husain	Zakir Hussain (tabla player)	**Zakir Hussain** is playing a *heart*-shaped tabla.
4.	Chair	V.V. Giri	V.V. Giri	**V.V. Giri** is sitting on a *chair*.
5.	Hook	Fakhruddin Ali Ahmed	Fake + rude + Alladin	**Fake** and **rude Alladin** is carrying a large *hook*.
6.	Hockey stick	Neelam Sanjiva Reddy	Neelam + Sanjiv + ready	**Neelam** and **Sanjiv** are **ready** with their *hockey stick*s.

7.	Axe	Giani Zail Singh	Giani + jail	President **Giani** is distributing *axe*s to the prisoners in **jail** for a new carpentry programme.
8.	Snowman	Ramaswamy Venkataraman	Rama + swami	Lord **Rama** has disguised himself as a **swami** to bless a *snowman*.
9.	Balloon	Shankar Dayal Sharma	Shankar (name of a boy)	Your friend **Shankar** is bursting *balloon*s.
10.	Bat + Ball	Kocheril Raman Narayanan	coach + Narayan (name of a boy)	**Narayan** is the **coach** of the *bat* and *ball* (cricket) team.
11.	Road	A.P.J. Abdul Kalam		
12.	Cap	Pratibha Patil		
13.	Butterfly	Pranab Mukherjee		
14.	Boat	Ram Nath Kovind		

Complete the table above by making the last four associations yourself. You may select your own images—those you find most suitable to be associated with the numbers.

Check your recalling power by answering the following questions:

1. **Who was the fifth President?** _____

   _____

   _____

2. **President Kocheril Raman Narayanan is at what number in the list?** _____

   _____

   _____

3. **Who was the President just before V.V. Giri?** _____

   _____

   _____

4. **Who was the President right after V.V. Giri?** _____

   _____

   _____

5. **President Pratibha Patil is at what number in the list?** _____

   _____

   _____

★★★

II. LANGUAGES

74

CHAPTER 14

★★★

IMPROVING VOCABULARY

Every now and then we come across new words in the English language through various mediums, like newspapers, books and the Internet. Many times we are unable to understand the gist of the topic because we don't understand the exact meanings of these new words. That's why it is important to expand your vocabulary, as it gives you an edge over others; however, learning new words can be a very challenging task.

One of the ways to build up your vocabulary is by using the PNN Method along with the AIR principle to strengthen our language skills.

Let's begin with some simple examples.

Example 1:

PUTRID *(adj.)* : If you see this word in a newspaper or a book, the first thing you do is look up its meaning. You find out that it means 'rotten'. Now, how will you remember this? Simple: you break up the word 'putrid' into 'put' + 'rid' and make an association with its meaning, which is 'rotten'. So imagine yourself **put**ting an apple into a dustbin to get **rid** of it as it is **rotten**.

The next time you see the word 'putrid' somewhere, an image of a rotten apple will flash through your mind. And after you come across this word a few times, it will automatically register in your mind, so you will be able to recall it and then use it. Let's look at some examples of the word's usage:

- The vegetables were left on the counter for too long and became **putrid**.
- The **putrid** smell coming from the drain led to several complaints by the residents.
- Eating **putrid** food will make you sick.

Example 2:

MEDIOCRE *(adj.)* : The meaning of this word is 'average' or 'neither good nor bad'.

Let's apply the PNN Method to this word:

'media' + 'car'.

This can then be memorized as 'I don't want to get into this **media car** as it is an **average** car.'

Let's apply the usage to some sentences:

- Arun is a **mediocre** basketball player—that's why he wasn't selected to be in the team.
- I was a **mediocre** student in school but became successful in my career.
- This movie got **mediocre** ratings from the critics.

Example 3:

<u>**ABUNDANT**</u> *(adj.)* : This means 'plentiful'.
Now apply the PNN Method: 'a' + 'bundle' + 'ant'.
You can visualize this as 'There is **a bund**le of **ant**s
on the lollipop.'

Let's apply the word to some sentences:

- We have **abundant** food at home; please join us for dinner.
- India has **abundant** reserves of coal.
- Mangoes are most affordable nowadays as the yield was **abundant** this year.

Example 4:

<u>**DAINTY**</u> *(adj.)*: This means 'delicately small and pretty'. After applying the PNN Method, we get: 'drain' + 'tea'.

You can visualize this using the following sentence: '**Drain** the **tea** into this **delicately small and pretty** cup.'

DRAIN THE TEA INTO THIS DELICATELY SMALL AND PRETTY CUP.

Now let's apply the usage to some sentences:

- The puppy's **dainty** ears looked cute.
- The venue was decorated with **dainty** flowers.
- We were served **dainty** little cakes at the party.

Example 5:

ABOLISH *(verb)* : The meaning of this word is 'to end'. And after applying the PNN Method, we get: 'a boy' + 'polish'. We can visualize this as: '**A boy** who shines shoes with shoe **polish** wants **to end** child labour.'

Let's look at the usage of the word:

- All the members of the committee were in favour of **abolishing** child labour in the state.
- The main objective of this non-profit organization is to **abolish** hunger and homelessness in the district.
- The new taxes on essential commodities need to be **abolished** as it burdens the citizens of the country.

★★★ LEARNING DIFFICULT WORDS ★★★
THROUGH THE PNN METHOD

Word	Meaning	PNN	Visualization
Adamant	Stubborn	ad(d) + a + man	The coach is **stubborn** about **add**ing **a man** to his team.
Miserable	Extremely unhappy	Mis(s) + able	**Miss** becomes **extremely unhappy** when she is not **able** to perform well in her drama class.
Privilege	Advantage	private + edge	The man had the **advantage** of having a **private edge** at the society's swimming pool.
Applaud	Clap	app + lord	The audience **clap**ped when an **app** to talk to the **lord** was launched.
Benign	Kind	bee + nine	**Bee**s are **kind** when they are in groups of **nine**.
Persuade	Convince	per(son) + suede	The **per**son **convince**d the model to wear a **suede** outfit even though it was very hot.
Repulsive	Extremely distasteful	re(peatedly) + pulses	It's **extremely distasteful** to **re**peatedly eat **pulses**.

Word	Meaning	PNN	Visualization
Massacre	Killing of a large number of people	mass + acre	Imagine a **mass** number of people being **kill**ed in an **acre** of land.
Mirth	Laughter	birth	The baby burst into **laughter** immediately after its **birth.**
Exorbitant	Very high	orbit + ant	The **orbit** of the Earth is full of **ant**s moving at a **very high** speed.

Now that you have learnt the memory technique to remember the meanings of new words, you can apply your knowledge and check your skill. Try making your own associations for the following words.

Word	Meaning	PNN	Visualization
Euphoria	Joy		
Picturesque	A beautiful place or a building		
Devastate	Destroy		
Subtle	Delicate		
Audacious	Daring		
Oblivious	Unaware		
Exert	Apply		
Elaborate	Detailed		
Forbid	Ban		
Atrocious	Terrible		

CHAPTER 15

LEARNING SPELLINGS

All of us have, at some point, faced difficulty in correctly spelling even the simplest English words. Many times it is because the word has repeated or silent letters in it. But there are techniques that make this easier. In this chapter, we will learn some amazing techniques that can make you an expert speller.

Let's start by looking at an example of a commonly misspelled and difficult word using the PNN Method. In this, we will look at both the correct and the wrong spellings, and visualize the right one.

Confusion between	:	Twelfth/Twelvth
Correct spelling	:	Twelfth
Visualization	:	*There is an **elf** hidden in tw**elf**th.*

As we learnt in the previous chapters, it is best to visualize hilarious scenarios, which will help you recall easily. Here, we imagine an elf, which is a supernatural creature that we often see in folk or fantasy tales.

Now, let's look at this table, which has more commonly misspelled words.

	Words	Correct word	Visualization
1.	Fascinate/Facinate	Fascinate	The boy is **fas**ting to fascinate the crowd.
2.	Discipline/Dicipline	Discipline	The **disc** is disciplined and stands in line.
3.	Beginning/Begining	Beginning	When I see others grinning, I begin to smile.
4.	Weird/Wierd	Weird	We will look weird if **we** fly like a **bird**.
5.	Apparent/Aparent	Apparent	This **app** is apparently famous.
6.	Guidance/Guidence	Guidance	The **guide** likes to **dance**.
7.	Imitation/Immitation	Imitation	There is no imitation of 'm'.
8.	Length/Lenth	Length	Let's add 'g' between 'n' and 't' to increase the length.
9.	License/Licence	License	The license was covered with **lice** but it still made sense.
10.	Quiet/Quite	Quiet	Be 'quiet' and silent about your 'diet'.
11.	Recommend/Recomend	Recommend	A double doze of 'm' is recommended.
12.	Secretary/Secretery	Secretary	My secretary has a **secret** diary.

13.	Sincerely/Sinceraly	Sincer**ely**	Do your work sincerely **since** we **rely** on you.
14.	Definite/Definate	Defi**nite**	It is definitely dark at **night** (nite).
15.	Familiar/Familier	Fami**liar**	You are familiar with the **liar**.
16.	Government/ Goverment	Gover**nm**ent	The 'n' leads 'm' in government.
17.	Humorous/ Humourous	Humorous	The 'u' in the middle is not humorous.
18.	Brilliant/Briliant	Bri**ll**iant	You are not brilliant if you neglect the 'l'.
19.	Pavilion/Pavillion	Pavi**l**ion	There is no space for two 'l's in this pavilion.

There's another technique that makes memorizing spellings easy. It's called an **acrostic**. In this method, we use each letter of the word as the first letter of a new word, and those words are used to make a meaningful sentence. Here, the first letter of each word reminds us of the correct spelling.

Let's look at some examples:

- ***Daughter***: **D**ear **A**unty **U**ses **G**ood **H**eels **T**o **E**nter **R**oom
- ***Rhythm***: **R**hythm **H**elps **Y**our **T**wo **H**ips **M**ove
- ***Laugh***: **L**augh **A**nd **U** **G**et **H**appy
- ***Carriage***: **C**arry **A** **R**ed **R**ibbon **I**n **A** **G**olden **E**gg
- ***Because***: **B**ig **E**lephants **C**an't **A**lways **U**se **S**mall **E**xits
- ***Ocean:*** **O**nly **C**ats' **E**yebrows **A**re **N**arrow

★★★ PRACTICE TIME ★★★

Try and make your own associations for the correct spellings of the given words.

	Words	Correct word	Association
1.	Acquit/ Aquit		
2.	Aggression/ Agression		
3.	Awful/ Awfull		
4.	Colum/ Column		
5.	Repetition/ Repitition		
6.	Vacuum/ Vaccuum		
7.	Precede/ Preceed		
8.	Scissors/ Scisors		
9.	Existence/ Existance		
10.	Independent/ Independant		

★★★

CHAPTER 16

HOMOPHONES

We once had two students in our class named Nikita and Nitika. Their names were a source of confusion for the rest of the students. To eliminate this mix-up, we asked the class to visualize Nikita (Niki) wearing a Nike t-shirt and Nitika (Niti) doing all her work with *niti*, which means 'the perfect way' in Hindi. This association removed all confusion.

In the English language, we face the same problem with certain words that have the same pronunciation but different spellings and meanings. These words are known as **homophones**. Let's look at some examples of these words and learn the best way to remember the correct spelling of each along with its meaning.

Let's start with this:

Here vs Hear

Here *(adverb)*: in, at or towards this place or position

Now let's see the usage of the word:

- Look **here**, I need to show you something.
- Come **here**! The exit is this way.
- The book that you were looking for is **here**.

Hear *(verb)*: to be aware of sound through the ear; to be told something

Let's now look at the usage of the word:

- I can **hear** you clearly!
- Did you **hear** that Anu is travelling to Europe?
- She **heard** me say I was hurt but she ignored me.

So how do you remember the spelling and its meaning? Through association:

Hear – You **hear** with your **ear**.
Here – **Here** is a place like **there** or **where**.

Let's learn how to differentiate between homophones by looking at some more examples.

	Word	Meaning	Association
1.	Aid	Help	The doctor gets p**aid** for the **aid**.
	Aide	Assistant	Your **aide** will always be by your s**ide**.
2.	Pair	Set of two	Birds can fly in the **air** with only a **pair** of wings.
	Pear	Fruit	We **ea**t p**ea**rs.
3.	Morning	Time of day	I **don't see** 'u' (you) in the **morning** because you get up late.
	Mourning	Feeling of sorrow	I can see that 'u' (you) are **mourning** because your cat died.
4.	Altar	A type of table in a church	The **altar** in the church has a **star**.

	Word	Meaning	Association
	Alter	Change	The dress will look better if you alter it.
5.	Pale	Light in colour	The pale dress was on sale.
	Pail	Bucket	He failed to fill the pail.
6.	Cue	Signal	The lifeguard got the cue to rescue the drowning girl.
	Queue	Line	People have to wait in queue to meet the queen.
7.	Discrete	Separate	Many discrete parts make this game complete.
	Discreet	Cautious	Be discreet while crossing the street.
8.	Compliment	Praise	She got many compliments when she climbed Mount Everest.
	Complement	Match	Lemon tea perfectly complements almond cake.
9.	Feat	Achievement	To eat this chilli is not an easy feat.
	Feet	Plural of foot	I can feel the cool waves on my feet.
10.	Idol	Statue	This idol is worth a million dollars.
	Idle	Inactive	There is little time to sit idle nowadays.

It is not always necessary to make associations for both the words. You can make an association for one of the words, which will help you distinguish its meaning from the other. For example, let's look at **naval** and **navel**. The difference in spellings is only the letters 'a' and 'e'. The meaning, however, is completely different. While nav**a**l is related to the navy, nav**e**l means 'belly button'. You can remember this using the sentence: *You will find your nav**e**l in your b**e**lly*.

This will automatically remind you to add an 'e' when you want to write about the body part and 'a' when you want it to relate to the navy.

Now let's have a look at **thrown** and **throne**.

Thrown is the past tense of throw. And a **throne** is the chair used by a monarch. You can differentiate and memorize these two words by remembering the following sentence:

*Only **one** person can sit on the thr**one**.*

★★★ PRACTICE TIME ★★★

Try and make your own associations to memorize the given homophones:

	Word	Meaning	Association
1.	Weather	Climate	
	Whether	Choice between options	
2.	Ascent	Rise/upward movement	
	Assent	Agree	
3.	Coarse	Rough	
	Course	Route	
4.	Forth	Forward	
	Fourth	Number four in a sequence	
5.	Accept	To receive	
	Except	To exclude	

★★★

HOMOPHONES

CHAPTER 17

LEARNING A FOREIGN LANGUAGE

Travelling to another country and meeting people from other nations is fairly common nowadays. Every now and then people travel to different countries for work, studies or leisure. Hence, it is important to know a few basic words in a foreign language. This is especially useful when you are travelling to another country and need to speak to the locals.

There are memory techniques that can help you memorize words in another language. Let's begin with some simple steps that you need to keep in mind.

Steps to follow:

Step 1: Find the meaning of the word you want to translate.
Step 2: Using the PNN Method, come up with a nickname for the word.
Step 3: Make a funny association between the two and visualize it clearly in your mind.

NOTE: THE PRONUNCIATION OF WORDS DIFFERS BASED ON ACCENTS. WE HAVE TO KEEP THIS IN MIND WHILE MAKING ASSOCIATIONS.

Let's look at a few French words.

Word	:	**Voiture**
Pronunciation	:	voi-chure
English Meaning	:	Car
PNN	:	vulture
Visualization	:	The *car* has many *vulture*s on top of it.

Word	:	**Lait**
Pronunciation	:	lay
English Meaning	:	Milk
PNN	:	late
Visualization	:	You are *late* to buy *milk*.

	French Word (pronunciation)	English Meaning	PNN	Visualization
1.	Argent (ahr-jean)	Money	urgent	You are in **urgent** need of **money** and are rushing to the bank.
2.	Affamé (affa-me)	Hungry or famished	after me	Come **after me** if you are **famished** (extremely **hungry**).
3.	Acheter (ashe-tey)	Buy	ashtray	You want to **buy** a beautiful **ashtray**.
4.	Je veux (zh-euveu)	I want	zoo + view	**I want** to go to the **zoo** to see the beautiful **view**.
5.	Un verre (a-where)	A glass	where	**Where** is the **glass**?
6.	Prix (pree)	Price	free	You ask the shopkeeper for the **price** of an item and he says it's for **free**.
7.	Autobus (auto-bus)	Bus	auto	All the **buses** in France are **auto**matic.
8.	Des magasins (day magga-zan)	Shops	day + magazine	Imagine a **shop** selling lots and lots of **magazine**s in one **day**.

9.	Pour homme (poor-om)	For men	poor + home	The government is making special **homes** for the **poor**, especially **for men** in rural areas.
10.	Marcher (mar-chey)	Walk	marching	You are **marching** on the beautiful **walk**ways in France.

Now let's look at some words in Italian.

★★★ VOCABULARY IN ITALIAN ★★★

Word	:	**Grazie**
Pronunciation:		grazie
English Meaning	:	Thank you
PNN	:	grazing
Visualization	:	A cow is *grazing* and saying, '*Thank you!*'

Word	:	**Bagno**
Pronunciation	:	ban-yo
English Meaning	:	Bathroom
PNN	:	ban + yo-yo
Visualization	:	*Yo-yos* are *ban*ned in the *bathroom*.

	Italian Word (pronunciation)	English Meaning	PNN	Visualization
1.	Per favore (pehr-fah voh-ray)	Please	pay + for + ray (stream of light)	**Please pay for** this **ray** of light. It is a very costly healing ray.
2.	Prego (pre-go)	You are welcome	please go	**You are welcome**d at your friend's house. **Please go** there.

3.	Sera (sera)	Evening	sir	**Sir** will come home in the **evening** to teach you Italian.
4.	Mattina (matt-tina)	Morning	mat + Tina	**Tina** sits on a **mat** every **morning** to do yoga.
5.	Pomeriggio (pomme-rigo)	Afternoon	pomegranate	Eating **pomegranate** in the **afternoon** is good for you.
6.	Notte (not-te)	Night	naughty	Kids become very **naughty** at **night**.
7.	Chi (ki)	Who	key	At the meeting, he asked, '**Who** is the **key** person here?'
8.	Quanto (quanto)	How much	Quantity	A shopkeeper is asking you **how much quantity** of Italian cheese you want.
9.	Aiuto (ai-you-toh)	Help	I + you + toe	**I** stepped on **you**r **toe** and you screamed, '**Help**!'
10.	Quando (quando)	When	condo	**When** are you shifting to your new **condo**?

Wasn't that fun to learn? Now let's crack some words in Spanish.

★★★ VOCABULARY IN SPANISH ★★★

Word : **Playa**
Pronunciation : play-ya
English Meaning : Beach
PNN : play
Visualization : Kids are *play*ing on the *beach*.

Word : **Carros**
Pronunciation : carros
English Meaning : Cars
PNN : carrots
Visualization : All the *cars* on the road are full of *carrots*.

	Spanish Word (pronunciation)	English Meaning	PNN	Visualization
1.	Casa (casa)	Home	castle	Your **home** in Spain is like a **castle**.
2.	Mercado (mer+cado)	Market	Mercedes + Rado	You have to go to the **market** to buy a **Mercedes** and a **Rado** watch.
3.	Teatro (tea-atro)	Theatre	tea	That **theatre** is famous for its **tea**.
4.	Estadio (estadio)	Stadium	studio	In Spain, **stadium**s are built like big **studio**s.
5.	Colegio (col-e-hio)	School	college	In Spain, **school**s are as big as **colleg**es.
6.	Azucar (a-zoo-car)	Sugar	a + zoo + car	You have to go to the **zoo** in **a car** to get **sugar**.
7.	Comida (comida)	Food	comedians	**Comedians** serve **food** in this new show.
8.	Pan de molde (pan de molde)	Bread	pan + mould	In Spain, **bread** is **mould**ed in a **pan**.

	Spanish Word (pronunciation)	English Meaning	PNN	Visualization
9.	Batidos (batidos)	Milkshakes	bat + dose	In this zoo, **bat**s are given **dos**es of **milkshakes**.
10.	Agua (ah-gua)	Water	guava	This **water** tastes like **guava**.

It's not that difficult, is it? Learning new words can be fun. It is also a unique skill. Now, let's move to German.

★★★ VOCABULARY IN GERMAN ★★★

Word : **Hasslich**
Pronunciation : hass + leash
English Meaning : Ugly
PNN : has + leech
Visualization : The man looked *ugly* as he *had leech*es crawling on his face.

Word	:	**Schön**
Pronunciation	:	shoon
English Meaning	:	Beautiful
PNN	:	shone
Visualization	:	She looked *beautiful* as the light *shone* on her face.

	German Word (pronunciation)	English Meaning	PNN	Visualization
1.	Heute (hoy-to)	Today	hot	It is **hot today**.
2.	Morgen (moh-gun)	Tomorrow	more + gun	**Tomorrow**, the soldiers will get **more gun**s for their training.
3.	Gestern (gestern)	Yesterday	guest + turn	The **guest** did not **turn** up **yesterday**.
4.	Weit (white)	Far	white	Everything looks **white** from **far** away.
5.	Lecker (lecker)	Tasty	(Boris) Becker	You like Germany for two reasons: the **tasty** food and tennis legend **Boris Becker**.
6.	Blume (bloo-muh)	Flower	bloom	**Flower**s **bloom**ed in all the fields in Germany.
7.	Gut (goot)	Good	gut	It is always **good** to follow your **gut** feeling.
8.	Koch (koh)	Chef/Cook	cough	The **chef** has a bad **cough**.

	German Word (pronunciation)	English Meaning	PNN	Visualization
9.	Zeit (zight)	Time	sight	In Germany, you can enjoy beautiful **sight**s all the **time**.
10.	Schwimmbad (schwim-bad)	Swimming pool	swim + bad	**Swim**ming is **bad** if the **swimming pool** is dirty.

Carefully follow these techniques and the examples taught in this chapter. You will be able to learn any new language with ease. So go ahead and try to learn some more words from different languages.

CHAPTER 18

HOW TO ACE PUBLIC SPEAKING

Addressing a large group of people is one of the biggest fears people have; even adults are often terrified of public speaking. The problem stems from the fear of forgetting what to say. However, this is a vital skill to have, and it is good to start practising when you're in school, as it is important to build confidence early on. Many students are afraid of giving speeches in front of their classmates at school functions or competitions. They fear they will forget the points of their speech and mess up in front of a large audience. In this chapter, we will learn how to apply the Hide and Seek Method to overcome this fear and ace public speaking. This method will not only help you remember your speeches but also make you more confident about your memory and oratory skills.

The Hide and Seek memory technique that you learnt earlier is probably one of the oldest memory methods in the history of the world. It is believed to have been used more than 2000 years ago by Roman debaters and speakers (also called orators). They presumably used this technique to visualize the key points of their speeches, thinking of a place or a room familiar to them (just like you did), and in a sequence. They too probably buried their information in these mental hiding places and then later used these to give their speeches with perfect accuracy.

So let's begin.

Say you are contesting an election for the post of house captain, and you have to give a presentation regarding your candidature in front of the whole school in your auditorium. Let's look at the speech you can give. Highlighted below are the key points.

1. I would like to be a part of the student's council so that I can take my **house to the top of the leaderboard.**
2. No effort will be spared by me to win the house **trophy**.
3. As you all know, I have been an active participant in many inter- and intra-school championships.
4. I have won the title of **Best Swimmer** since the sixth standard and have also represented the school at the **zonal and state levels**.
5. Winning the **Best Athlete Award** in 2017 is another one of my achievements.
6. I have been actively taking part in **dramatics**.
7. My keen interest in photography led me to the position of the secretary of the **Photography Club**, and I have represented the school at inter-school movie-making and photography events.
8. I will ensure that every student gets an **equal opportunity** to participate, without any bias.
9. It will give me great pride to **serve my house**, and I will take full ownership of all the **responsibilities** I will be entrusted with.

10. I am sure my hard work, willingness to participate in every competition, love for the house and

enthusiasm will take this house to greater heights. So please **vote for me and show your support.**

Thank you!

You can memorize the key points of the speech by associating them with some hiding places in the auditorium itself. Taking a sequential route of the auditorium, mark some hiding places in your mind, such as:

1. **Door**
2. **Speakers**
3. **Fans**
4. **Stairs of the stage**
5. **Podium**
6. **Stage**
7. **Mahatma Gandhi's framed portrait**
8. **Flower pot**
9. **Bottles of water**
10. **Audience**

You can make the associations between the key points and hiding places as follows:

1. **Door** – Visualize a house on top of the *door*.
2. **Speakers** – Visualize that a trophy is kept on the *speaker* and you are making every effort to reach it.
3. **Fans** – Now, see yourself participating in various championships on the wings of the *fan*.
4. **Stairs of the stage** – See yourself swimming on the *stairs*— zonal level on the lower stair and state level on the upper stair.
5. **Podium** – Visualize yourself getting an award and medal for Best Athlete on the *podium*.

6. **Stage** – See yourself playing the lead role in a drama on *stage*.

7. **Mahatma Gandhi's framed portrait** – Imagine that people are taking photographs of *Mahatma Gandhi's framed portrait*.

8. **Flower pot** – Visualize yourself giving an equal number of *flowers* to every student, thereby giving equal opportunities to all.

9. **Bottles of water** – Visualize yourself telling your schoolmates, 'Trust me, this *water* is pure. Thank you for giving me the responsibility of serving my house.'

10. **Audience** – Imagine that students in the *audience* are very enthusiastic and promising to support and vote for you.

While giving your speech, just look around the auditorium in sequence, from the door to the audience, and recite your lines confidently. You'll notice that if you apply this method, you will not miss a single point, as each hiding place will remind you of the points in your speech. Good luck!

III. SOCIAL SCIENCE

CHAPTER 19

SELECTING THE BEST TECHNIQUE FOR LONG ANSWERS

As you get promoted to higher standards and grades, you'll notice that your textbooks contain more information about topics and you'll be required to write longer answers. Now, memorizing multiple points on a theme or topic can be difficult, be it history or science. But you are required to learn and retain them. The techniques in this book will teach you how to memorize long answers in simple ways, and in this section of the book we will tackle some of these. One way of remembering long answers is to use the following steps:

1. Just break your long answers into small sentences.
2. Take a key word from each sentence.
3. Associate the words using the Chain Method, or use any of the peg systems: the Hide and Seek Method, the Rhyme Method or the Shape Method. Here, the hiding places or number images serve as pegs to hold or associate the information to be memorized.
4. You can paint a mental picture of that association (using the PNN Method, if required).

5. And finally, while recalling, just remember the pegs and you will be able to write the whole answer correctly without missing a single point.

We will look at various examples from different subjects in the coming chapters. After studying them, **try the same method for a few long answers of any subject** of your choice. Choose the ones that you find difficult to remember. If you find it intimidating, first try with shorter ones before graduating to the longer answers. You'll see that in no time you will be able to ace all the once-problematic long answers. All you need to do is practise.

★★★ HOW TO CHOOSE THE BEST METHOD ★★★

Now we come to how to find and select the method that works best for each kind of academic question. If you have trouble remembering short answers, then the **Chain Method** is the best technique to follow, as you just need to associate one piece of information with the next in a chain sequence.

For long answers, the **Hide and Seek Method** is more useful, as the number of hiding places is unlimited (this is handy because long answers have more key words), and even if you miss out one point in the middle, you can recollect the other points with accuracy, unlike the Chain Method, in which a broken link may not let you recall two to three points.

When information needs to be memorized in sequence, the peg methods, like the **Rhyme Method** and the **Shape Method**, have an advantage over the others. Irrespective of the method you use, after strongly visualizing the associations in your mind two to three times, the answers will be embedded in your memory.

Revising answers that have been memorized using these methods doesn't take much time.

However, it all depends on you and which methods you are most comfortable with in the end. All the methods are equally helpful in memorizing different kinds of answers, but you need to choose which method works best for you. You may sometimes choose a combination of various methods. In the coming chapters you will find lots of examples of the same. So try all the methods and select those that suit your needs best.

CHAPTER 20

TACKLING LONG ANSWERS
IN SOCIAL SCIENCE

In the last chapter we learnt the technique behind memorizing long answers. In this chapter we will practically apply a combination of various memory techniques to memorize long answers in a subject like social science. We will be looking at long answers in geography and history in particular; however, the technique you learn in this chapter can be applied to answers in any subject. Let's start!

★★★ PART 1 – GEOGRAPHY ★★★

Q1: What are the ways to conserve land?

Ans:

Land can be conserved in the following ways:

1. **Afforestation**
2. Planting of shelter **belts of plants**
3. Control on **overgrazing**
4. Stabilization of sand dunes by growing **thorny bushes**
5. Proper management of **wastelands**
6. Control of **mining** activities

7. **Proper discharge and disposal of industrial effluents and wastes** after treatment can reduce land and water degradation in industrial and suburban areas.

(Source: NCERT, Class X, Social Science, Contemporary India II)

The Memory Solution:

The keywords in the answer are highlighted. We are using the Chain Method here to memorize the keywords. Let us visualize the points:

1. Imagine a dense forest.
2. Cattle are grazing on belts of plants.
3. But we need to control overgrazing.
4. So thorny bushes are planted.
5. That resulted in wastelands.
6. Mines are found under wastelands.
7. Industries are built on top of mines and their waste is being properly treated before discharge and disposal.

Q2: What is the land use pattern in India?
Ans:
1. Use of land is determined by human factors—population, density, technological capability, culture and traditions.
2. It is determined by physical factors—topography, climate and soil.
3. The total geographical area of India is 3.28 million sq. km.
4. The land under permanent pastures has decreased, which has made cattle feeding difficult.

5. Other than current fallow lands, most land is either of poor quality or the cost of cultivation is high. Hence, these lands are cultivated once or twice every two to three years, and if these are included in the net sown area (NSA), then the percentage of NSA in India comes to about 54 per cent of the total reporting area.

6. The pattern of NSA varies from state to state. It is 80 per cent of the total area of Punjab and Haryana and less than 10 per cent in Arunachal Pradesh, Mizoram, Manipur and the Andaman and Nicobar Islands.
7. Forest area is less than 33 per cent of geographical area.
8. Land put to other non-agricultural uses includes settlements, roads, railways and industry.
9. A part of the land is termed wasteland, which includes rocky, arid and desert areas.

(Source: NCERT, Class X, Social Science, Contemporary India II)

The Memory Solution:

So, how do we learn this answer? We will make use of the **Hide and Seek Method** to associate the points and the **Phonetic Method** to convert numbers into images.

Let us picture the land use pattern in India as a piece of land on which a residential society or complex is located. Now, let's undertake a journey through the complex to spot hiding places for our key points.

Some of the hiding places in a society can be:

1. **Guard room**
2. **Fountain**

3. **Society map**
4. **Tennis court**
5. **Road**
6. **Different buildings of the society**
7. **Swimming pool**
8. **Shopping centre**
9. **Parking**

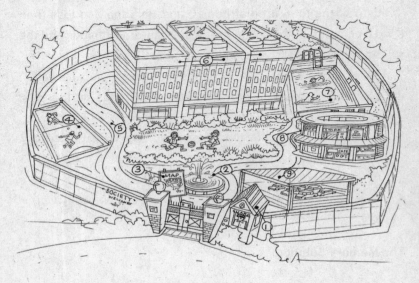

Let's understand the memory solution. We can see that the use of land is determined by many things, such as:

1. **Human factors**—population, density, technological capacity, culture and traditions.
   The memory clue here can be the **Guard room**. Visualize the guard telling you at the gate that the population in this society is densely technological but rich in culture and traditions.
2. **Physical factors**—topography, climate, soil.
   Memory Clue: **Fountain**.

Among the physical features of the society, the fountain is a top priority (topography), as it makes the climate cool and the soil fertile.

3. The total geographical **area** of India is **3.28 million** sq. km.
Memory Clue: **Society map**.
A girl named Milli (million) is saying, 'See my (3) knife* (28)? The total area is mine.'

4. The land under **permanent pastures** has **decreased**, which has made **cattle feeding difficult.**
Memory Clue: **Tennis court**.
Due to the construction of a tennis court, permanent pastures have decreased, and it is difficult for the cattle of the society to feed.

5. Other than current fallow lands, most land is either of **poor quality or the cost of cultivation is high**. Hence, these lands are cultivated once or twice every two to three years, and if these are included in the NSA, then the percentage of NSA in India comes to about 54 per cent of the total reporting area.
Memory Clue: **Road**.
The roads are of poor quality and the cultivation cost is high, so cultivation is done on it once or twice every two to three years.

6. The pattern of NSA varies from state to state. It is **80 per cent** of the total area of **Punjab and Haryana** and less than **10 per cent** in **Arunachal Pradesh, Mizoram, Manipur and the Andaman and Nicobar Islands**.
Memory Clue: **Different buildings of the society**.
The residential building in which the people of Punjab and Haryana are living has poor electricity, and the fuse* (80 per cent) is always out. Now visualize watching a boy named Arun (Arunachal) buying a Maaza (Mizoram), the mango drink, with

10 per cent of his money (Manipur) to drink on an island (Andaman and Nicobar Islands).

7. **Forest area** is less than **33 per cent** of the geographical area.

   Memory Clue: **Swimming pool**.

   Mam˙ (33) is explaining that due to the large swimming pool, the forest area is very little.

8. Land put to other non-agricultural uses includes settlements, roads, railways and industry.

   Memory Clue: **Shopping centre**.

   Land in the shopping centre is put to non-agricultural uses, like settlements, roads, railways and industry.

9. A part of the land is termed **wasteland**, which includes rocky, arid and desert areas.

   Memory Clue: **Parking**.

   Wasteland, which includes rocky, arid and desert areas, is used for parking.

★★★ PART 2 – HISTORY ★★★

Q3: What were the areas of conflict between the Bengal nawabs and the East India Company that led to the Battle of Plassey?
Ans:

The following are the areas of conflict between the nawabs of Bengal and the East India Company:

- Siraj ud-Daulah, as the nawab of Bengal and one of the strongest rulers, refused to grant the company concessions; demanded large tributes for the company's right to trade;

˙ Numbers are converted into images using phonetic codes. For these phonetic codes, refer to Chapter 9: Phonetic Peg System.

denied it the right to mint coins; and stopped it from extending its fortification.

- Accusing the company of deceit, the nawab claimed that the company was depriving the Bengal government of huge amounts of revenue and undermining his authority.

- The company was refusing to pay taxes, writing disrespectful letters, and trying to humiliate the nawab and his officials.
- The company on its part declared that the unjust demands of the local officials were ruining the trade of the company, and trade could flourish only if the duties were removed.
- The company was also convinced that in order to expand trade it had to enlarge its settlements, buy up villages and rebuild its forts. The conflicts led to confrontations and finally culminated in the famous Battle of Plassey.

(Source: NCERT, Class VIII, Our Past III)

The Memory Solution:

To understand and memorize the areas of conflicts between the company and the nawab of Bengal, you can visualize that you are watching a play called *The Battle of Plassey*. We are making use of the PNN Method and the Chain Method to depict the play.

Imagine the scene being enacted on stage right now is of the *darbar* of Nawab Siraj ud-Daulah. British officials of the East India Company are standing in the traders' chamber, asking for permission to trade in the nawab's region, Bengal, and Siraj ud-Daulah is giving them some conditions:

1. They will get no concession, coin minting or fortification (CCF).

2. They will have to pay large tributes (LT).

Imagine the next scene—the nawab is accusing the company of deceit as they have not given him a receipt of their revenues, thus depriving him of a huge amount of money and also undermining his authority.

He has also got hold of disrespectful letters written by the company to humiliate him and his officials.

Now, the next scene. In their defence, the company is presenting the following points:

1. Demands of officials are seen as unjust and unfair
2. No taxes
3. Removal of trade duties

They are also planning to buy more villages and forts to expand trade. However, the nawab is not agreeing to their conditions.

Now, picture an escalation of the argument, which invariably leads to the **Battle of Plassey**.

Q4: What led to battles between different European trading companies in the seventeenth century, and how were battles fought between them?

Ans:

The following are the reasons that led to battles between trading companies:

- The problem was that all the companies were interested in buying the same things.
- The fine-quality cotton and silk produced in India had a big market in Europe. Pepper, cloves, cardamom and cinnamon too were in great demand.
- Competition amongst the European companies inevitably pushed up the prices at which these goods could be purchased, and this reduced the profits that could be earned.
- The only way trading companies could flourish was by eliminating rival competitors.
- The urge to secure markets led to fierce battles between the trading companies.
- Battles were fought by regularly sinking each other's ships and blockading routes.
- This prevented rival ships from moving with supplies of goods.
- Trade was carried out with arms and weapons, and trading posts were protected through fortification.

(Source: NCERT, Class VIII, Our Past III)

The Memory Solution:

Now that you have looked at the answer, let's visualize the situation and connect the above points one by one using the Chain Method, which will make this easier to learn.

1. Visualize that many trade representatives from different European companies have come to your local market to purchase goods from two famous shops.

2. One shop is selling fine-quality cotton and silk fabrics and the other shop is selling spices like pepper, cloves, cardamom and cinnamon.

3. The products are of such great quality that all the companies want the same items from the two shops. Because of this great demand, the two shopkeepers have now increased the prices.

4. Traders want to eliminate their competitors, as that will lead to more profits and they'll flourish.

5. This leads to fierce battles between different trading representatives.

6. Visualize now that the goods are being transported in ships. However, to create trouble for their competitors, trading companies are sinking each other's ships, blocking their routes and preventing their movement.

7. The traders employ bodyguards, who carry arms and weapons to fortify them.

Now you must have understood how to easily memorize long answers in social science subjects. The techniques discussed in this chapter can be extended to various combinations of other methods, like the Shape Method and the Rhyme Method along with the PNN Method. Also, they can be used not just for long answers in social science but also for other subjects like science, economics and business studies.

The creative and hilarious visualizations will help you look at memorizing long answers in a new light.

CHAPTER 21

HISTORY DATES

History is a great subject but memorizing the dates of historical events can be intimidating for many. These numerous dates often create a phobia within us like no other. With memory techniques, however, we can make this task easy and full of fun. We do this by using a combination of various mnemonics learnt in the previous chapters.

To memorize dates of historical importance, we need to form a mental image of the historical event and that of the date. Then we need to create those images by understanding the following steps.

★★★ STEPS TO MEMORIZE HISTORY DATES ★★★

1. Visualize the event:
First, visualize the historical event that needs to be memorized, like the birth of Mahatma Gandhi or the beginning of the First World War, using the PNN Method.

2. Visualize the date:
A date consists of three parts—*date*, *month* and *year*.

    (a) Dates can be visualized using the number peg system: Dates ranging from 1 to 20 can be memorized using the Shape Method.

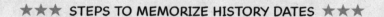

Dates ranging from 21 to 31 can be memorized using the Rhyme Method, where the codes for 1 to 11 can be used for the dates 21 to 31 of any month. For example, one (sun) can be used for 21, two (shoe) can be used for 22, and so on.

(b) Months can be given images that have associations with some important day, event or occasion occurring in that month. Here are some related images you can associate these months with:

MONTHS	IMPORTANT EVENT/DAY	IMAGES
January	Beginning of the new year	New Year party
February	Valentine's Day	Rose
March	Holi	People playing with colours
April	April Fools' Day	Joker
May	International Workers' Day	Workers working in a factory
June	Summer vacation	Holiday on a beach
July	Rainy season/ Monsoon	Umbrella
August	Independence Day	National flag
September	Teachers' Day	Teacher
October	Gandhi Jayanti	Mahatma Gandhi
November	Children's Day	Children playing
December	Christmas	Santa Claus

If a particular month reminds you of some other important event from your life or from history, you can associate its image accordingly.

(c) Years can be memorized by converting the year into images using the phonetic peg system.

(d) If the century is 1900 or 2000, then you don't need to add anything extra to it. For other centuries, you may use the following colour codes:

Years	Colour Codes
1500	Yellow
1600	Brown
1700	Royal blue
1800	Fluorescent green

It's totally your choice what colour you want to give to a particular century, as long as you keep it constant throughout.

3. Make the association:

The third step in memorizing dates is visualizing an association between the event and the date.

Let's look at some examples to make things clear:

1. **Date of birth of Prime Minister Narendra Modi – 17 September 1950**

    17: Sandwich *(Shape Method)*

    September: Teacher

    19**50**: Lays *(Phonetic Method)*

The confusion here could be about the year and not the century, so there is no need to convert the century in dates like this.

Visualization: After the birth of **Prime Minister Narendra Modi**, all **teachers** *(September)* were given a party, and **sandwiches** *(17)* and **Lays** *(1950)* chips were served.

2. **Terrorist attack at the Taj Mahal hotel in Mumbai – 26 November 2008**
   26: Sticks *(Rhyme Method)*
   November: Children
   2008: **S**ofa *(Phonetic Method)*
   Visualization: Many children were sitting on a **sofa** *(2008)* in the lobby of the **Taj Mahal hotel** when it was attacked by terrorists with **sticks** *(26)*.

3. **Battle of Plassey – 1757**
   Battle: Fight
   Plassey: Glass
   1700: Blue *(century code)*
   57: **L**a**k**e *(Phonetic Method)*
   Visualization: Into a **blue lake** *(1757)*, a crystal **glass** *(Plassey)* fell, and everybody began **fighting** to take it out.

4. **First Anglo Maratha War – 1775–1782**
   Maratha: Shivaji
   1700: Blue *(century code)*
   75: Cool *(Phonetic Method)*
   82: **f**a**n** *(Phonetic Method)*
   Visualization: **Shivaji** landed the first blow on his enemy with a big **blue cool fan** *(1775–1782)*.

5. **The death of Alivardi Khan and the succession of Siraj ud-Daulah as the next nawab of Bengal – 1756**

   Alivardi Khan: Alivardi Khan

   Siraj ud-Daulah: Sir + Raju + Allah

   1700: Blue *(century code)*

   56: lee**ch** *(Phonetic Method)*

   Visualization: A blue **leech** *(1756)* bit **Alivardi Khan** and he died. After his death, **Sir Raju** prayed to **Allah** and he was made the nawab of Bengal.

6. **Napoleon became the emperor of France – 1804**

   1800: Green *(century code)*

   04: **s**i**r** *(Phonetic Method)*

   Visualization: When **Napoleon** became **emperor**, his **sir** *(1804)*, the commanding officer, placed a crown—which had a big **green** stone on it—on his head.

7. **Napoleon was defeated at the Battle of Waterloo – 1815**

   Waterloo: Water in hot loo

   1800: Green *(century code)*

   15: **d**oll *(Phonetic Method)*

   Visualization: Napoleon was attacked and defeated by a small **doll** *(1815)* wearing a **green** dress while he was looking for **water in** a **hot loo**.

8. **Birth of Gautam Buddha – 563 BC**

   563: **Leg**u**m**e *(Phonetic Method)*

   Visualization: After the birth of **Gautam Buddha**, his father distributed **legumes** to everyone.

9. **Hindi was made the official language of India – 26 January 1965**

26 January: Republic Day

1965: **Jail** *(Phonetic Method)*

Visualization: As part of the celebrations in **jail** *(1965)* for **Republic Day** *(26 January)*, **Hindi** was announced as the official language of India.

10. **Death of Aurangzeb – 1707**

1700: Blue *(century code)*

07: **sky** *(Phonetic Method)*

Visualization: Aurangzeb fell from the **blue sky** and died.

11. **First English factory set up on the banks of the River Hugli – 1651**

Hugli: Hugging

1600: Brown *(century code)*

51: **lud**o *(Phonetic Method)*

Visualization: The first **English factory** is being established on the banks of a river, and people are **hugging** *(Hugli)* each other and playing **ludo** *(1651)* on the **brown** sand.

Now let's look at some important dates related to sports:

1. **First Asian Games in India – 1951**

1951: **Lud**o *(Phonetic Method)*

Visualization: When the **Asian Games** were held for the first time in India, the event was inaugurated by playing **ludo** *(51)*.

2. **Khashaba Dadasaheb Jadhav became the first Indian to win an individual Olympic medal in wrestling – 1952**

Khashaba: Cash + bow

1952: **Li**on *(Phonetic Method)*

Visualization: You are telling a **lion** *(1952)*, 'I will earn a lot of **cash** when you take a **bow** after winning the Olympic medal.'

3. **Mihir Sen was the first Asian to swim across the English Channel – 1958**

    Mihir: My + hero

    1958: **L**eaf *(Phonetic Method)*

    Visualization: Mihir is **my hero** because he crossed the English Channel on a **leaf** *(1958)*.

4. **Six sixes in an over by Yuvraj Singh against England – 2007**

    2007: **Sk**y *(Phonetic Method)*

    Visualization: Yuvraj Singh batted six sixes in the **sky** (07) against England.

5. **Abhinav Bindra won India's first individual Olympic gold medal – 2008**

    2008: **S**ofa *(Phonetic Method)*

    Visualization: When **Abhinav Bindra** won a gold medal at the Olympics for shooting, he was brought from the airport on a **sofa** (08).

Now practise some history dates by yourself:

1. Battle of Buxar – 1764

Hint:

_____

_____

2. Viswanathan Anand wins the FIDE World Chess
    Championship – 2000

_____

_____

3. Saina Nehwal wins a bronze medal at the Olympics – 2012

   _____

   _____

4. Sachin Tendulkar becomes the first batsman in the world to make 100 international centuries – 2012

   _____

   _____

5. Birth date of Subhas Chandra Bose – 23 January 1897

   _____

   _____

★★★

IV. BIOLOGY

CHAPTER 22

MEMORY APPLICATION TO SCIENCE: DEFECTS IN VISION

When applying memory techniques, it is not always necessary to make associations for the whole answer, especially when we have to memorize the differences (of characteristics and features) between two things. In such cases, it is enough to memorize only the characteristics of one out of two, as logically you would know that the other is just the reverse of the first. For example, this can be applied when you're learning about metals and non-metals, concave and convex lenses, acids and bases, or animals and plants, where most of the characteristics of one are just the opposite of the other. This works very well while learning answers in pure sciences, like biology, chemistry and physics, where we have to remember information about two or more things. In this chapter we will use memory methods to recollect information from your biology books. Let's understand it by taking an example of two common defects in vision.

Q: Distinguish between myopia and hypermetropia. How can these visual defects be corrected?

Ans:

MYOPIA

Myopia means short-sightedness. A person suffering from this defect can see nearby objects clearly but distant objects appear blurred. The image of a distant object is formed in front of the retina. This defect is due to a decrease in focal length of the eye lens or elongation of the eye ball. To correct this defect, spectacles with concave lenses of the required power are used.

HYPERMETROPIA

Hypermetropia means long-sightedness. A person suffering from this defect can see distant objects clearly but nearby objects appear blurred. The image of a nearby object is formed behind the retina. This defect is due to an increase in focal length of the eye lens or the eye ball becoming too small. To correct this defect, spectacles with convex lenses of the required power are used.

(Source: NCERT, Science textbook, Class X)

To learn the defects of vision, we first write the differences between the two in tabular form and highlight the keywords as shown below. This will make it easier for us to memorize the answer.

	MYOPIA	HYPERMETROPIA
1.	Short-sightedness	Long-sightedness
2.	A person can see **nearby objects clearly** but distant objects appear blurred.	A person can see **distant objects clearly** but nearby objects appear blurred.

	MYOPIA	HYPERMETROPIA
3.	**Image** of distant object is formed in **front of the retina**.	**Image** of nearby object is formed **behind the retina**.
4.	This defect is due to a **decrease in focal length** of eye lens or **elongation of the eye ball**.	This defect is due to an **increase in focal length** of eye lens or the **eye ball** becoming **too small**.
5.	To correct this defect, spectacles with **concave lenses** of the required power are used.	To correct this defect, spectacles with **convex lenses** of the required power are used.

The Memory Solution:

Visualize that *Maya* (**Myopia**) is a girl who is *short* (short sightedness), which is why she is able to see objects at a *short* (nearby) *distance*. However, she cannot see objects at a *long* (distant) *distance* as a big *rat* (retina) keeps coming in front of her whenever she is trying. Due to this, she *loses focus* and her *eyeballs become long*. So she needs to wear *spectacles* (lens) that are kept in a long *cave* (concave).

NOTE: IT IS NOT NECESSARY TO VISUALIZE A SIMILAR SITUATION FOR HYPERMETROPIA AS IT IS JUST THE OPPOSITE OF MYOPIA. HOWEVER, IF YOU WANT TO MAKE AN ASSOCIATION, YOU CAN MAKE A PNN OF HYPERMETROPIA, LIKE 'METRO RAIL', AND THEN VISUALIZE THE KEY POINTS OF THE CHARACTERISTICS OF HYPERMETROPIA BY ASSOCIATING THEM WITH 'METRO RAIL' USING THE CHAIN METHOD AND THE PNN METHOD AS DONE EARLIER.

Now practise the same to memorize the differences between plant and animal cells.

	PLANT CELL	ANIMAL CELL
1.	Plant cells are larger than animal cells.	Animal cells are generally smaller.
2.	Rigid cell wall is present.	Cell wall is absent.
3.	Nucleus lies on one side of the cell.	Nucleus lies in the centre of the cell.
4.	Plastids are present.	Plastids are absent.
5.	Large and few central vacuoles are present.	Small and numerous central vacuoles are present.
6.	Cilia are absent.	Most contain cilia.
7.	Centrosomes are absent.	Centrosomes are present.

To memorize the differences above, it is enough to visualize the characteristics of any one kind of cell—that will remind you of the characteristics of the other, as they are exactly opposite in nature. Also, it is not necessary to connect the points with the Chain Method. You could use any of the peg methods, such as the Rhyme Method or the Shape Method to associate your points of information with the number pegs or hooks.

★★★

CHAPTER 23

LEARNING DIAGRAMS: ANIMAL CELL

Diagrams play a very important role in pure sciences. They not only make the concept easier to understand but also fetch you more marks in your examinations. Memory techniques help you form a clear image of diagrams in your mind while associating them with their relevant details. For example, let us take a diagram with all its characteristics and use the PNN Method and the Chain Method to form a story.

Here are the main characteristics of an animal cell:

1) The cell membrane is semi-permeable; it allows only specific materials to enter.
2) The cytoplasm is a jelly-like substance that provides a surface for all the organelles in the animal cell.
3) The nucleus is the control centre of the cell, and it decides and controls most of the functions going on in the cell.
4) Mitochondria are sites for cellular respiration in cells. They are also called the powerhouses of the cell because they release energy-rich components called ATP.
5) ATP is needed for the functioning, growth and maintenance of the body.

6) The endoplasmic reticulum is a large network of membrane sound sheets. It helps in transporting and exchanging materials between various regions of the cytoplasm. It's of two types: SER and RER.

7) Smooth endoplasmic reticulum (SER) helps in the formation of lipids. Lipids are essential components of the cell membrane.

8) Rough endoplasmic reticulum (RER) has ribosomes. Ribosomes help build protein in the RER.

9) The proteins go to the Golgi apparatus. They are processed inside the Golgi apparatus. They are packed and sent out. The Golgi apparatus is involved in the formation of lysosomes.

10) Lysosomes contain powerful digestive enzymes that help digestion. When the cell is damaged, lysosomes burst. After the lysosomes burst, digestive enzymes get released, which digest their own cell. This is why lysosomes are the suicide bags of the cell.

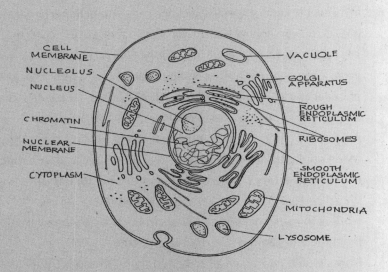

LEARNING DIAGRAMS: ANIMAL CELL

The Memory Solution:

Let's look at the memory solutions to visualize the points above and learn the answer.

1. You can visualize an animal cell like a big factory that is surrounded by a boundary wall (**cell membrane**). Not everybody can enter the factory. Only those who have an entry pass can enter (*semi-permeable*).

2. As you enter, your feet get stuck to some sticky substance on the floor. This is **cytoplasm**, which is a *jelly-like substance* spread on the floor of the factory. That's why you are provided with special shoes. On this floor are placed various machines called *organelles*.

3. In the centre, there is an office that is the **control centre** of the cell. The director of the factory, called the **nucleus**, sits in it. The nucleus *decides and controls most of the functions* going on in the factory.

4. In the whole factory are oval sections called **mitochondria**, which provide power (light/might) to the whole factory. This is why they are called *powerhouses* of the factory. Everybody practises the yoga technique pranayama (**respiration**) there, which releases an **energy-rich component called ATP**. This is needed for *functioning, growth and maintenance* of the factory workers.

5. Around the central office (**nucleus**), there are large benches made of plastic sheets. These sheets are called **endoplasmic reticulum (a large network of membrane bound sheets)**. Visualize that there are some people sitting on these. Their work is to *transport and exchange* materials between various machines (**organelles**) in the factory (**cell**).

6. Now picture two types of benches there: **smooth (SER)** and **rough (RER)**. The smooth ones are soft like lips (**formation**

of lipids), whereas the rough ones are rough because thorny ribs (**ribosomes**) are embedded in them. The ribs (**ribosomes**) are helping in the *synthesis of proteins*.

7. These proteins go into the next machine, which looks like a golf ball and is called the **Golgi apparatus**. Here, *processing* and *packaging of proteins* is done. However, along with this, lice (**lysosomes**) are also formed as a byproduct.

8. The lice (**lysosomes**) produced contain *powerful digestive enzymes*. When the factory (**cell**) is damaged, the lice burst out and digestive enzymes get released, which digest the whole factory. That is why they are also called the *suicide bags* of the cell.

You will realize that with this method you remember not only the diagram but also the characteristics of its components. Follow this method using your imagination to remember similar diagrams and concepts.

CHAPTER 24

PLANT KINGDOM AND ANIMAL KINGDOM

In this chapter, we will discuss how to memorize the classifications of the plant and animal kingdoms using the PNN Method and the Chain Method.

Living organisms have been classified into five broad categories. These are also called the five kingdoms. Their names are:

1. **Kingdom Monera**
2. **Kingdom Protista**
3. **Kingdom Fungi**
4. **Kingdom Plantae**
5. **Kingdom Animalia**

Amongst these, Plantae and Animalia kingdoms are larger than the others. They are further divided into various divisions based on different criteria. Science students are required to memorize all these levels of classification as well as the difficult terminologies used in these classifications. In this chapter, we will try to go through this information and memorize it.

★★★ PLANT KINGDOM ★★★

Let's start with Kingdom Plantae. The classification of the plant kingdom can be represented in the form of the flow chart given below:

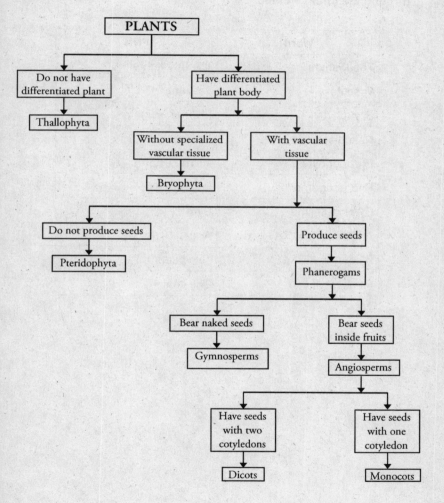

(Source: NCERT – Science textbook of Class IX)

The Memory Solution:

As we can see, there are various difficult terminologies used in the above plant classification, so we will use the PNN Method to convert these terms into images that can be easily memorized through the Chain Method.

Word	PNN
Thallophyta	The low fighter
Vascular	Vaseline
Bryophyta	Brother + fight
Naked seeds	Naked seeds
Pteridophyta	Terror + fight
Phanerogams	Fun games
Gymnosperms	Gym
Angiosperms	Angel
Dicots	Two coats
Monocots	One coat

The Memory Solution:

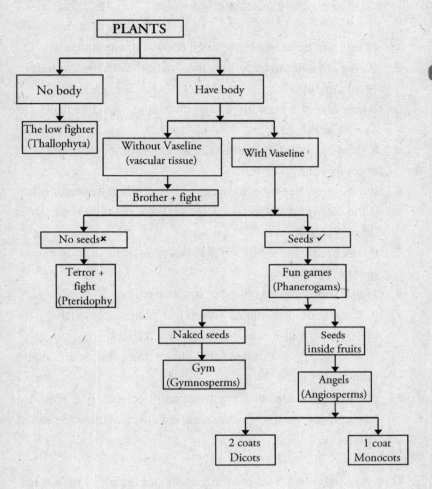

(Source: NCERT – Science textbook of Class IX)

As you can see, the words have become quite easy now, so let's look at the simplified associations below:

1. Plants can be of two types: with body and without body.
2. If they are without body, they have to fight with the low fighter (thallophyta).
3. If they are with body, they can either apply Vaseline (vascular tissue) or not.
4. If they do not apply Vaseline, then the brother will fight with them (bryophyta).
5. If they apply Vaseline, they can either produce seeds or not.
6. If the plants do not produce seeds, they will fight with terror (pteridophyta).
7. If they produce seeds, then they have fun while playing games (phanerogams).
8. These seeds can be naked or inside a fruit.
9. If the seeds are naked, then the plants go to the gym (gymnosperms).
10. If the seeds are inside the fruit, they become angels (angiosperms).
11. If the angels are wearing two coats (cotyledons), they are called 'dicots' and if they are wearing one coat, they are called 'monocot'.

This may seem like a lot of information, but once you read it two to three times and try to visualize it clearly, it will remain in your memory for a longer time.

Now we move on to Kingdom Animalia, which we will learn in the same way as we did for the plant kingdom.

★★★ ANIMAL KINGDOM ★★★

The main classifications of the animal kingdom are:

- **Porifera**
- **Coelenterata**
- **Platyhelminthes**
- **Nematoda**
- **Mollusca**
- **Annelida**
- **Arthropoda**
- **Echinodermata**
- **Protochordata**
- **Vertebrata:** Pisces, Amphibia, Reptilia, Aves, Mammalia

The classification above, with its difficult names and pronunciations, would be difficult for most of us to remember, but by using memory techniques, we can easily memorize this. Let's first use the PNN Method and then make a story out of the words. Look at the word associations below:

Word	PNN
Animal Kingdom	Pet animals
Porifera	Porridge
Coelenterata	Calendar
Platyhelminthes	Plate
Nematoda	Nemo (the famous clownfish from the Disney movie *Finding Nemo*)

Word	PNN
Mollusca	Mall
Annelida	Anaconda
Arthropoda	Earth + powder
Echinodermata	Ache + no + matter
Protochordata	Proteins
Vertebrata	Vertebrae
Pisces, Amphibia, Reptilia, Aves, Mammalia	**PARAM** Veer Chakra

Now we can make a story using the words above. Let's begin in order:

❖ One morning, I was giving my **pet animals** *(animal kingdom)* some **porridge** *(porifera)*, when the **calendar** *(coelenterata)* on the table grabbed my eye. I remembered that I had to go to the market to purchase **plates** *(platyhelminthes)*.

❖ I took my fish, **Nemo** *(nematoda)*, and went to a **mall** *(mollusca)* to shop for these.

❖ There I saw that a giant **anaconda** *(annelida)* was digging up the **earth** and making a **powder** *(arthropoda)* of it.

❖ This powder would remove all **aches, no matter** *(echinodermata)* what.

❖ So I bought it, and all my aches disappeared, as the powder contained lots of **proteins** *(protochordata)*.

❖ And these proteins provided strength to my **vertebrae** *(vertebrata)*.

❖ For the strongest vertebrae, I imagined myself being awarded the **PARAM** Veer Chakra. *(PARAM is an acronym for **P**isces, **A**mphibia, **R**eptilia, **A**ves, **M**ammalia.)*

Apart from memorizing the names of the classified groups, students are also required to remember their respective characteristics. So let's take a look at the characteristics of coelenterata.

The characteristics of coelenterata are:

a) These are **animals living in water**.
b) They show more **body-design differentiation**.
c) There is a **cavity** in the body.
d) They are **diploblastic**.
e) Some live in **colonies,** while others are **solitary**.
f) Some examples of coelenterata are **jellyfish, hydras and sea anemones**.

The Memory Solution:

The bold words are the keywords, which can be visualized using the PNN Method and the Chain Method, as follows:

- Coelenterata: *calendar*
- Animals living in water: *animals in water*
- Body-design differentiation: *different body designs*
- Cavity: *cave*
- Diploblastic: *double blast*
- Colonies: *colonies or groups*
- Solitary: *solitaire*
- Sea anemone: *sea animals*

Move on to the visualization now:

Imagine that you have an amazing *calendar* on your table. As you turn it, you see it has pictures of various *animals living in water*, and you can even see them moving! Many *jellyfish*, *hydras* and other *sea animals* are there. They all have *different designs* on their bodies. Then you notice that they are going into a big *cave*. Suddenly, you hear *double blasts* from inside the cave. Some animals hide in *colonies* (groups), while some lucky others find a *solitaire*.

What did you think about this visualization? Let's try another one.

Below are the characteristics of nematoda:

a) They are **bilaterally symmetrical**.
b) They are **triploblastic**.
c) They have **cylindrical** bodies.
d) There are **tissues** but no real organs.
e) **Pseudocoelom** is present.
f) They are known as **parasitic worms**, causing diseases such as **elephantiasis**.
g) Some examples are the **wuchereria** and the **ascaris**.

The Memory Solution:

Nematoda: *Nemo from* Finding Nemo.

- Bilaterally symmetrical: *beautifully symmetrical*
- Triploblastic: *blasts three times*
- Cylindrical: *cylinder*
- Tissues: *tissue paper*
- Pseudo coelom: *sweet column*
- Parasitic worms: *parasitic worms*
- Elephantiasis: *elephant*
- Wuchereria: *voucher*
- Ascaris: *scary*

Now visualize using the above points:

Picture that *Nemo* the clownfish is *beautifully symmetrical*. He swims into a *cylinder*, which *blasts three times*, and something icky comes out of it. He wipes himself with a *tissue paper* and hides in a *column of sweets*. There he is chased by *parasitic worms* that cause diseases in *elephants*. Strangely, they give Nemo a *voucher* instead, but he finds it quite *scary*.

Using the same method, you can memorize the characteristics of other classified groups in science.

V. CHEMISTRY

CHAPTER 25

MEMORIZATION IN CHEMISTRY: LEARNING THREE OR MORE TOPICS

Across all the subjects in your curriculum, you'll be required to have in-depth knowledge about a particular topic or a theme. This means that the questions in the chapter might be related to each other or overlap in some way. When there are three to four questions related to each other in the same chapter, we can memorize them all together by forming a long chain or by using several hiding places. In this chapter, through chemistry, we will see how we can learn different things about the same topic without forgetting the key points. Here we will be using three questions from the topic 'Coal and Petroleum', which we will memorize through a single journey using the Hide and Seek Method and the PNN Method.

Q1: Give the uses of coal and also list the various products obtained from it.

Ans: Coal is used as a fuel to cook food; as a fuel in various industries; and as a source of thermal power to produce electricity. It is processed to obtain useful materials like:
1.   Coke – A type of fuel that is used in the manufacture of steel. Also used in the extraction of other metals.

2. Coal Gas – Used for cooking, heating and lighting.
3. Coal Tar – Used in making synthetic dyes, drugs, perfumes, paints and roofing material.

Q2: List the products obtained from petroleum refining along with their uses.

151

Ans: The following products are acquired from petroleum refining:

1. Liquefied petroleum gas (LPG) – Used as fuel for home and industry.
2. Petrol – Used as a fuel in automobiles. Also used as a solvent in dry cleaning.
3. Kerosene – Used as a fuel in lamps and stoves.
4. Diesel – Used as a fuel in heavy motor vehicles. Also used in electric generators.
5. Fuel oil – Used at power stations and ships.
6. Lubricating oil – Used for lubrication in heavy machines.
7. Paraffin wax – Used to make candles, wax, ointment and Vaseline.
8. Asphalt – Used for making roads.

Q3. What are the uses of natural gas?

Ans: Natural gas is used in the following:

1. For the generation of electricity.
2. Compressed natural gas (CNG) is used as a fuel in automobiles as it is more environmentally friendly.
3. As a domestic fuel, transported to houses via gas pipelines.
4. In the production of ammonia and hydrogen.
5. In the manufacture of steel, glass, plastics and other products.

(Source for all questions: NCERT – Science textbook for Class VIII)

MEMORIZATION IN CHEMISTRY: LEARNING THREE OR MORE TOPICS

The Memory Solution:

We can use the Hide and Seek Method to memorize the answers above. As we learnt in the previous chapters, we can create different hide-and-seek places. Here is a sample route map, where we look at hiding places in the route from a house to a metro station:

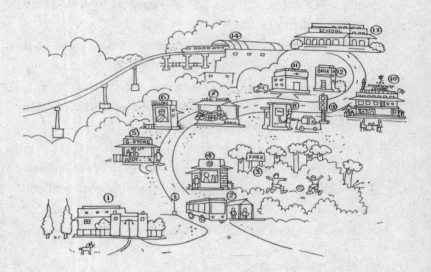

The hiding places in the image above are:

1. **House**
2. **Bus stop**
3. **Park**
4. **Milk dairy**
5. **General store**
6. **Salon**
7. **Vegetable shop**
8. **Petrol pump**
9. **Traffic signal**

10. Community centre
11. Hospital
12. Bank
13. School
14. Metro station

We can memorize all three long answers on this journey, one followed by the other. Let's make associations between the hiding places and the points of answers:

1. **Coal** – Let's associate this with the house.
   You are using coal to cook food in your house, and your father is using it in his factory as fuel. Visualize your plants (thermal power plants) producing electricity.

2. **Coke** – Next, the bus stop.
   Visualize that at the bus stop, everybody is served Coke (the drink) in steel glasses. Some people are using their own glasses, which are made from other metals.

3. **Coal gas** – We visualize a park next.
   Picture that in the park, one person is burning coal in a corner to get fuel for cooking, heating and lighting lamps for his shop.

4. **Coal tar** – We move on to the milk dairy.
   You see black coal tar present in the milk sold at the dairy. Since the milk has gone bad, it is being used to make synthetic dyes, drugs and paints. The remaining coal tar is used as roofing material for roof of the dairy.

5. **LPG** – Next is the general store. You reach the general store and see that along with other things, the store is selling LPG cylinders for homes and industries.

6. **Petrol** – Then comes the salon.

All petrol automobiles are parked outside the salon, and you notice that along with haircuts, customers are given free dry cleaning.

7. **Kerosene –** We associate this with the vegetable shop.

    You see the vegetable shopkeeper arriving at his shop in a jet. You see him filling it with kerosene, as kerosene is a very cheap fuel for his jet. He also uses it to light his stove and lamps at the shop.

8. **Diesel –** We connect this to the petrol pump.

    You see many heavy motor vehicles queuing up at the petrol pump to buy diesel. In one corner, a man is filling diesel in an electric generator.

9. **Fuel oil –** We link this to the traffic light.

    Visualize yourself at the traffic light; you see it turning red, and suddenly all the leftover fuel is converted into oil, which is used in power stations and ships.

10. **Lubricating oil –** We associate this with the community centre.

    Picture that in the community centre are big machines that are being oiled with lubricating oil.

11. **Paraffin wax –** Connect this to the hospital.

    Visualize that paraffin wax is used in the hospital to make wax, candles, ointment and petroleum jelly for the patients.

12. **Asphalt –** Associate this with the bank.

    Imagine that the officials at the bank are making a road in front of their branch. However, due to a lack of training, they make a grave fault (asphalt), which ruins the road.

13. **Natural gas –** Connect this word to the school.

    Visualize that the school is celebrating Natural Gas Day and is promoting its positive uses. You take a tour of the school and locate some new places, like the parking lot, reception, classrooms, chemistry lab and kitchen. Visualize all the points you read in the natural gas answer and connect them to these places.

- **Parking** – Visualize that teachers are only allowed to buy CNG cars, as they are environmentally friendly.
- **Reception** – Electricity for the whole school is produced in the reception area using natural gas.
- **Classrooms** – Natural gas is transmitted to each classroom via gas pipelines.
- **Chemistry lab** – Natural gas is used to produce ammonia and hydrogen.
- **Kitchen** – Various utensils of steel, glass and plastic are made from natural gas.

How did you like these visualizations? Did it make learning the long answers easier for you? These answers are fairly easy to understand; however, due to an overlap of information (since all of them are related to fuels), some of you might get confused while memorizing their uses. In the memory method above, you might find that some points are repeated, but you won't get confused because when you visualize them in different and distant places, it becomes easy to register in the brain.

CHAPTER 26

★★★

THE PERIODIC TABLE-I

The periodic table is an arrangement of all the elements known to man in accordance with their increasing atomic number and recurring chemical properties. The first ninety-four elements of the periodic table are naturally occurring, while those from ninety-five to 118 have only been synthesized in laboratories or nuclear reactors.

Recalling all the elements of the periodic table is difficult given the sheer number of them. However, every student is required to memorize these names along with other information associated with them. No matter how hard you try, perfect recollection cannot be guaranteed by rote memorizing.

In this chapter we will learn how to remember difficult facts with the help of memory techniques using the imagination and creativity of the brain.

★★★ MEMORIZING THE PERIODIC TABLE ★★★

There are 118 elements in the periodic table.

And if you know the codes of the phonetic peg system well, you can memorize the entire periodic table in just a day or two.

Sounds impressive, doesn't it? Yes, it's very much possible! Hundreds of our students have mastered this.

HOW CAN ONE DO IT?

To learn the periodic table, one can convert the abstract names of elements into images by using the PNN Method. To learn atomic numbers, the phonetic peg system is used, and you can keep referring to the previous chapters for it. Once you have images for both the element and the atomic number, you need to make a funny association between them so that you can recall them easily.

Some examples:

a) The atomic number of **lithium** is **03**

   Lithium   – Lychee (PNN Method)

   03   – **S**u**M**o (Phonetic Method)

Visualization: The ***sumo*** *wrestler is eating lots of* ***lychees***.

b) The atomic number of **phosphorus** is **15**

   Phosphorus – Fox (PNN Method)

   15   – **D**ol**L** (Phonetic Method)

*Visualization: The **fox** is playing with a **doll**.*

c) The atomic number of **argon** is **18**

Argon — Gun (PNN Method)

18 — **D**war**F** (Phonetic Method)

*Visualization: The **dwarf** is playing with a toy **gun**.*

d) The atomic number of **vanadium** is **23**

Vanadium — Van (PNN Method)

23 — **N**ee**M** (Phonetic Method)

*Visualization: A **van** is stuck on top of the **neem** tree.*

Now let's look at the chart below that has the atomic numbers of many other elements. This will help you memorize the complete periodic table:

Elements (Symbol)	Atomic No.	PNN of element	Phonetic Codes (At. No.)	Associations
Hydrogen (H)	01	Hydrogen bomb	SuiT	The magician converted the **hydrogen bomb** into a beautiful **suit**.
Helium (He)	02	Heel	SuN	High **heels** are required to walk comfortably on the surface of the **sun**.
Lithium (Li)	03	Lychee (fruit)	SuMo	The **sumo** wrestler is eating lots of **lychees**.
Beryllium (Be)	04	Berry	SiR	**Sir** is carrying a large bag full of **berries**, so you ask him if he needs help.
Boron (B)	05	Boar	SaLe	He took his pet **boar** to visit the grand **sale** that was taking place at the mall.
Carbon (C)	06	Car + bun	SaGe	The **sage** is in deep meditation while sitting on top of a big **bun** on the roof of a **car**.
Nitrogen (N)	07	Night	Sky	The **sky** is black at **night**.
Oxygen (O)	08	Ox	SoFa	An **ox** is dancing funnily on the **sofa** in your living room.

Elements (Symbol)	Atomic No.	PNN of element	Phonetic Codes (At. No.)	Associations
Fluorine (F)	09	Floor	SoaP	Everybody in your family is slipping as there is a lot of **soap** on the **floor**.
Neon (Ne)	10	Knee	DoSa	Everyone at the party was served **dosa**, but they had to bend their **knees** in order to eat.

Visualize the above associations clearly two to three times to familiarize yourself with them and strengthen them in your brain. Then, proceed to the associations below. Here, you will learn how to memorize the next forty elements of the periodic table.

Elements (Symbol)	Atomic No.	PNN of element	Phonetic Codes (At. No.)	Associations
Sodium (Na)	11	Soda water	DaD	**Dad** is drinking cold **soda water** with his juice on this hot day.
Magnesium (Mg)	12	Maggi	DeN	You and your friends are cooking **Maggi** in the **den** on your trekking trip as it is raining outside.
Aluminium (Al)	13	Alum (chemical compound)	DaM	**Alum** is used to purify the water in the **dam**.

Elements (Symbol)	Atomic No.	PNN of element	Phonetic Codes (At. No.)	Associations
Silicon (Si)	14	Silly person	Dr	You visit your general practitioner and find him dancing in the room. Your dad says, 'This **Dr** looks absolutely **silly**.'
Phosphorus (P)	15	Fox	DolL	The **fox** is playing with a **doll**.
Sulphur (S)	16	Cell with fur	DiSH	Researchers discovered a new kind of **cell** that has **fur** all around it. For the exhibit, they displayed it in a **dish**.
Chlorine (Cl)	17	Clown	DecK	Everybody is watching a **clown** dance on the **deck**.
Argon (Ar)	18	Gun	DwarF	The **dwarf** is playing with a toy **gu**n.
Potassium (K)	19	Pot	TaP	A big earthen **pot** that has a **tap** attached to it is in great demand this summer.
Calcium (Ca)	20	Calcium tablet	NoSe	Scientists have invented a **calcium tablet** that can be inhaled through the **nose**.

Elements (Symbol)	Atomic No.	PNN of element	Phonetic Codes (At. No.)	Associations
Scandium (Sc)	21	Candy	NeT	You keep all your **candy** in a special **net** that is hidden in your room.
Titanium (Ti)	22	Titan	NuN	The **nun** is wearing a **Titan** watch.
Vanadium (V)	23	Van	NeeM	A **van** is stuck on top of the **neem** tree.
Chromium (Cr)	24	Crow	NehRu (Prime Minister Jawaharlal Nehru)	You see an old photograph of Prime Minister Jawaharlal **Nehru**, in which a **crow** is flying around him.
Manganese (Mn)	25	Magnet	NaiL	You buy a packet of **magnets** that are shaped like **nail**s.
Iron (Fe)	26	Iron Man	NaCHo (snack)	In the newest **Iron Man** comic, the superhero increases his power by eating **nachos**.
Cobalt (Co)	27	Bald	NecK	My **bald** friend has a long **neck**.
Nickel (Ni)	28	Pickle	NiFe (knife)	Your father made you chop all the **pickle**s with a **knife**.

Elements (Symbol)	Atomic No.	PNN of element	Phonetic Codes (At. No.)	Associations
Copper (Cu)	29	Cop	NiPpo	The **cop** uses only **Nippo** batteries in his torch.
Zinc (Zn)	30	Jinn	MesS	The **jinn** is serving food in the **mess** very quickly.
Gallium (Ga)	31	Gal	MaT	The **gal** is sitting on a colourful **mat** in the theatre.
Germanium (Ge)	32	Germs	MooN	The news says that all the **germs** on earth are flying to the **moon**.
Arsenic (As)	33	Scenic	MaM	**Mam** is taking us to a **scenic** place for a picnic.
Selenium (Se)	34	Sell	aaMiR	**Aamir** Khan is **selling** books based on his movies.
Bromine (Br)	35	Broom	MaiL	All the students are confused as someone sent a **broom** through the **mail** to the school address.
Krypton (Kr)	36	Corrupt	MatCH (stick)	According to a new study, **corrupt** people always carry loose **match**sticks in their pockets.

Elements (Symbol)	Atomic No.	PNN of element	Phonetic Codes (At. No.)	Associations
Rubidium (Rb)	37	Ruby (gem)	MiKe	At the concert, the singer's **mike** was decorated with beautiful red **rubies**.
Strontium (Sr)	38	Straw	M.F. (Husain)	The auction house is selling **M.F. Husain's** painting that was made using **straw** instead of brushes.
Yttrium (Y)	39	Yeti	MaP	While on holiday, you see that a **yeti** has lost its way and is looking at a **map**.
Zirconium (Zr)	40	Zircon	RoSe	Your friend gifts you a **rose** that is decorated with **zircon**s.
Niobium (Nb)	41	New bombs	RaT	Scientists are developing **new bombs** that make **rats** do crazy dances.
Molybdenum (Mo)	42	Mobile + denim	RaiN	In the **rain**y season, people use **mobile** covers made of **denim**.

Elements (Symbol)	Atomic No.	PNN of element	Phonetic Codes (At. No.)	Associations
Technetium (Tc)	43	Technician	RaM	In this new movie, Lord **Ram** becomes a **technician** to solve everyone's problems.
Ruthenium (Ru)	44	Ruth (a person's name)	ReaR	One should **rear** animals with **Ruth** because she is great at taking care of them.
Rhodium (Rh)	45	Road	RaiL	People are talking about a new **rail**way line that runs on the **road** instead of on tracks.
Palladium (Pd)	46	Podium	RiDGe	Students are lifting the **podium** to take it to the **ridge**.
Silver (Ag)	47	Silver	RacK	You gave your parents **rack**s that were made of **silver**.
Cadmium (Cd)	48	Cadbury	RooF	**Cadbury** chocolates are hanging from the **roof** of my house.

Elements (Symbol)	Atomic No.	PNN of element	Phonetic Codes (At. No.)	Associations
Indium (In)	49	Indian	RoPe	The **Indian rope** trick is very famous.
Tin (Sn)	50	Tintin	LayS (chips)	**Tintin** is busy eating **Lays** chips.

Study the above visualizations and try to recall the atomic numbers of the following elements:

Element	Symbol	At. No.
Sodium	Na	
Lithium	Li	
Nitrogen	N	
Phosphorus	P	
Potassium	K	
Carbon	C	
Chlorine	Cl	
Neon	Ne	
Silicon	Si	

★★★ PRACTICE TIME ★★★

Now try to make your own associations for the remaining elements with their atomic numbers:

Element	Symbol	Atomic No.	PNN of element	Phonetic Codes (At. No.)	Association
Antimony	Sb	51		LuDo	
Tellurium	Te	52		LioN	
Iodine	I	53		LiMe	
Xenon	Xe	54		LaRa (Brian)	
Cesium	Cs	55		LiLy	
Barium	Ba	56		LeeCH	
Lanthanum	La	57		LaKe	
Cerium	Ce	58		LeaF	
Praseodymium	Pr	59		LaB	
Neodymium	Nd	60		JuiSe	
Promethium	Pm	61		JeT	
Samarium	Sm	62		JeaN(s)	
Europium	Eu	63		JaM	
Gadolinium	Gd	64		JaR	
Terbium	Tb	65		JaiL	
Dysprosium	Dy	66		JudGe	
Holmium	Ho	67		JacKy (Chan)	
Erbium	Er	68		J.F. (jelly fish)	
Thulium	Tm	69		JeeP	
Ytterbium	Yb	70		KisS	
Lutetium	Lu	71		KiTe	
Hafnium	Hf	72		KoNe (cone)	

Element	Symbol	Atomic No.	PNN of element	Phonetic Codes (At. No.)	Association
Tantalum	Ta	73		KoMb (comb)	
Tungsten	W	74		KaR (car)	
Rhenium	Re	75		KoaL (coal)	
Osmium	Os	76		KaSH (cash)	
Iridium	Ir	77		KaKe (cake)	
Platinum	Pt	78		KoFee (coffee)	
Gold	Au	79		KaP (cap)	
Mercury	Hg	80		FuSe	
Thallium	Tl	81		FeeT	
Lead	Pb	82		FaN	
Bismuth	Bi	83		F.M. (radio)	
Polonium	Po	84		FiRe	
Astatine	At	85		FiLe	
Radon	Rn	86		FiSH	
Francium	Fr	87		FoK (fork)	
Radium	Ra	88		FiFa	
Actinium	Ac	89		F.P. (fountain pen)	
Thorium	Th	90		BuS	
Protactinium	Pa	91		BaT	
Uranium	U	92		BuN	
Neptunium	Np	93		BoM (bomb)	
Plutonium	Pu	94		BeaR	
Americium	Am	95		BelL	
Curium	Cm	96		BuSH	
Berkelium	Bk	97		BiKe	

Element	Symbol	Atomic No.	PNN of element	Phonetic Codes (At. No.)	Association
Californium	Cf	98		B.F (best friend)	
Einsteinium	Es	99		BaBy	
Fermium	Fm	100		ToSS	
Mendelevium	Md	101		ToaST	
Nobelium	No	102		DiSNey	
Lawrencium	Lr	103		TeaSe Him	
Rutherfordium	Rf	104		TuSsaR (silk)	
Dubnium	Db	105		DieSeL	
Seaborgium	Sg	106		DoSaGe	
Bohrium	Bh	107		DeSK	
Hassium	Hs	108		DoZe ofF	
Meitnerium	Mt	109		DSP (police)	
Darmstadtium	Ds	110		TaTtooS	
Roentgenium	Rg	111		Tata Tea	
Copernicium	Cn	112		Titan	
Nihonium	Nh	113		sTaDiuM	
Flerovium	Fl	114		TwiTteR	
Moscovium	Mc	115		ToTaL	
Livermorium	Lv	116		Tight Jaw	
Tennessine	Ts	117		aTTiC	
Oganesson	Og	118		DaTiVe	

CHAPTER 27

★★★

THE PERIODIC TABLE-2

The periodic table is divided into groups (columns), in which the elements in each group behave similarly while bonding with other elements, and periods (rows), in which elements in one period have the same number of electron shells. Dmitri Mendeleev, widely referred to as the father of the periodic table, put forth the first iteration of the periodic table, which is similar to the one we use now.

In this chapter, we will learn how to memorize the set of elements in different groups by making a simple sentence using *acrostic mnemonics.* An acrostic is a type of mnemonic, in which the first letter of each word or term is taken and used to form new words that make a meaningful sentence or phrase. We also need to associate the sentence with the corresponding group number. The group numbers are given images using the Phonetic Method. So we make these associations for each group.

S-Block Elements:

Consisting of the first two groups, s-block elements have similar physical and chemical properties. The valence electrons of the elements in this block occupy s-orbitals.

Group 01:

Symbol	Elements	Sentence
H	Hydrogen	**H**idden
Li	Lithium	**Li**nk (road)
Na	Sodium	**S**hould
K	Potassium	**P**ass
Rb	Rubidium	**R**adiant
Cs	Cesium	**C**ountry
Fr	Francium	**Fr**ance

Sentence: **H**idden **L**ink road **S**hould **P**ass **R**adiant **C**ountry **Fr**ance
Association: A person wearing a red **suit** *(01)* is going to France via the hidden link road.

Group 02:

Symbol	Elements	Sentence
Be	Beryllium	**Be**rries (in)
Mg	Magnesium	**M**aggi
Ca	Calcium	**C**ause
Sr	Strontium	**St**rong
Br	Barium	**Br**own
Ra	Radium	**R**ashes

Sentence: **B**erries in **M**aggi **C**ause **S**trong **B**rown **R**ashes
Association: Eating berries in Maggi while standing in the **sun** *(02)* causes strong brown rashes.

P-Block Elements:

Consisting of the last six groups of the periodic table (groups 13 to 18), p-block elements have their valence electrons occupying p-orbitals. This block consists of non-metals, semi-metals and poor metals.

Group 13:

Symbol	Elements	Sentence
B	Boron	**B**ring
Al	Aluminium	**A**ll
Ga	Gallium	**G**ems
In	Indium	**I**nto
Tl	Thallium	**T**hailand

Sentence: **B**ring **A**ll **G**ems **I**nto **T**hailand
Association: Collect all the gems from the **dam** *(13)* and bring them into Thailand.

Group 14:

Symbol	Elements	Sentence
C	Carbon	**C**all
Si	Silicon	**S**illy
Ge	Germanium	**G**erms
Sn	Tin	**T**o
Pb	Lead	**L**ab

Sentence: **C**all **S**illy **G**erms **T**o **L**ab
Association: The **Dr** *(14)* is calling silly germs to his lab.

Group 15:

Symbol	Elements	Sentence
N	Nitrogen	**N**ight
P	Phosphorus	**P**hotos
As	Arsenic	**A**re
Sb	Antimony	**A**nyway
Bi	Bismuth	**B**eautiful

Sentence: **N**ight **P**hotos **A**re **A**nyway **B**eautiful
Association: A photo shoot for a **doll** *(15)* is taking place, and her night photos seem more beautiful than those taken in the day.

Group 16:

Symbol	Elements	Sentence
O	Oxygen	**O**xygen
S	Sulphur	**S**upplier
Se	Selenium	**S**ells
Te	Tellurium	**T**elephone
Po	Polonium	**P**oles

Sentence: **O**xygen **S**upplier **S**ells **T**elephone **P**oles
Association: A **dog** *(16)* is supplying oxygen and selling telephone poles to hang the oxygen cylinders from.

Group 17:

Symbol	Elements	Sentence
F	Fluorine	**F**ull
Cl	Chlorine	**C**loud
Br	Bromine	**B**urst
I	Iodine	**I**n
At	Astatine	**A**ssam

Sentence: **F**ull **C**loud **B**urst **I**n **A**ssam

Association: From the **deck** *(17)*, people are watching a full cloudburst in Assam.

Group 18:

Symbol	Elements	Sentence
He	Helium	**H**is
Ne	Neon	**N**eon
Ar	Argon	**A**rt
Kr	Krypton	**K**reated
Xe	Xenon	e**X**tra
Rn	Radon	**R**ays

Sentence: **H**is **N**eon **A**rt **K**reated e**X**tra **R**ays

Association: The **dwarf** *(18)* filled his artwork with neon colours, which are creating extra rays.

D-Block Elements:

D-block elements consist of the element groups 3 to 12, which correspond to the filling of the d-orbital sub shell of the second outermost shell.

Group 03:

Symbol	Elements	Sentence
Sc	Scandium	**S**can
Y	Yttrium	**Y**eti's
	Lanthanides Series	**L**engthy
	Actinides Series	**A**ction

Sentence: **S**can Yeti's Lengthy Action
Association: Scan the yeti's lengthy actions through this **sim** *(03)*.

Group 04:

Symbol	Elements	Sentence
Ti	Titanium	**T**itan's
Zr	Zirconium	**Z**ircons
Hf	Hafnium	**H**alf
Rf	Rutherfordium	**R**ubber

Sentence: **T**itan's **Z**ircons **H**alf **R**ubber
Association: **Sir** *(04)* purchased a beautiful Titan watch but found that half of its zircons were made of rubber.

Group 05:

Symbol	Elements	Sentence
V	Vanadium	**V**endor's
Nb	Niobium	**N**ew
Ta	Tantalum	**T**ent
Db	Dubnium	**D**umped

Sentence: **V**endor's **N**ew **T**ent **D**umped

Association: A vendor purchased a new tent on **sale** *(05)*, but its quality was not good, so he dumped it.

Group 06:

Symbol	Elements	Sentence
Cr	Chromium	**C**row
Mo	Molybdenum	**M**ay
W	Tungsten	**T**urn
Sg	Seaborgium	**S**weet

Sentence: **C**row **M**ay **T**urn **S**weet

Association: This crow speaks bitterly, but I believe in the company of a **sage** *(06)*, it may turn sweet.

Group 07:

Symbol	Elements	Sentence
Mn	Manganese	**M**agazines (and)
Tc	Technetium	**T**echnology
Re	Rhenium	**R**emove
Bh	Bohrium	**B**oredom

Sentence: **M**agazines and **T**echnology **R**emove **B**oredom
Association: Flying in the **sky** *(07)* is very boring, but magazines and technology, like my mobile and tablet, remove my boredom.

Group 08:

Symbol	Elements	Sentence
Fe	Iron	**I**ron
Ru	Ruthenium	**R**ich
Os	Osmium	**O**rganic
Hs	Hassium	**H**erbs

Sentence: **I**ron **R**ich **O**rganic **H**erbs
Association: The **sofa** *(08)* is full of packets containing iron-rich organic herbs.

Group 09:

Symbol	Elements	Sentence
Co	Cobalt	**C**abs on
Rh	Rhodium	**R**oad
Ir	Iridium	**I**rritate
Mt	Meitnerium	**M**other

Sentence: **C**abs on **R**oad **I**rritate **M**other
Association: A man is washing cabs on the road with **soap** *(09)*, and that is irritating my mother.

Group 10:

Symbol	Elements	Sentence
Ni	Nickel	**N**ick
Pd	Palladium	**P**olishes
Pt	Platinum	**P**latinum
Ds	Darmstadtium	**D**rums in stadium

Sentence: **N**ick **P**olishes **P**latinum **D**rums in stadium

Association: Nick likes to eat **dosas** *(10)* while polishing his platinum drums in the stadium.

Group 11:

Symbol	Elements	Sentence
Cu	Copper	**C**opper
Ag	Silver	**S**hines like
Au	Gold	**G**old
Rg	Roentgenium	**R**ing

Sentence: **C**opper **S**hines like **G**old **R**ing

Association: **Dad** *(11)* bought a ring made of copper, which shines like a gold ring.

Group 12:

Symbol	Elements	Sentence
Zn	Zinc	**Z**inn
Cd	Cadmium	**C**odes
Hg	Mercury	**M**ercedes
Cn	Copernicium	**C**opyright

Sentence: **Z**inn **C**odes **M**ercedes **C**opyright
Association: Zinn went inside the **den** *(12)* to code the Mercedes copyright.

Repeat and clearly visualize the above sentences two to three times to strengthen their impression in your brain. After that, visualize each one's association with its respective group number, as given above. While recalling, phonetic codes will help you recall the group number and the sentence associated with it.

Periodic Table of Elements

| 1 H Hydrogen 1.00794 | 2 | | | | | | | Key: Atomic Number, Symbol, Element, Atomic weight |

1	2	3	4	5	6	7	8	9
1 H Hydrogen 1.00794								
3 Li Lithium 6.941	**4** Be Beryllium 9.01218							
11 Na Sodium 22.9897	**12** Mg Magnesium 24.305							
19 K Potassium 39.098	**20** Ca Calcium 40.078	**21** Sc Scandium 44.956	**22** Ti Titanium 47.867	**23** V Vanadium 50.941	**24** Cr Chromium 51.996	**25** Mn Manganese 54.938	**26** Fe Iron 55.847	**27** Co Coba Coba 58.93
37 Rb Rubidium 85.4678	**38** Sr Strontium 87.62	**39** Y Yttrium 88.906	**40** Zr Zirconium 91.225	**41** Nb Niobium 92.906	**42** Mo Molybdenum 95.94	**43** Tc Technetium (98)	**44** Ru Ruthenium 101.07	**45** Rh Rhod 102.9
55 Cs Cesium 132.9054	**56** Ba Barium 137.327	**57** *La Lanthanum 138.905	**72** Hf Hafnium 178.49	**73** Ta Tantalum 180.947	**74** W Tungsten 183.84	**75** Re Rhenium 186.207	**76** Os Osmium 190.23	**77** Ir Iridiu 192.2
87 Fr Francium (223)	**88** Ra Radium (226)	**89** †Ac Actinium (227)	**104** Rf Rutherfordium (261)	**105** Db Dubnium (262)	**106** Sg Seaborgium (266)	**107** Bh Bohrium (264)	**108** Hs Hassium (269)	**109** Mt Meitn (268)

*Lanthanide Series

58 Ce Cerium 140.116	59 Pr Praseodymium 140.907	60 Nd Neodymium 144.24	61 Pm Promethium (145)	62 Sm Samarium 150.36	63 Eu Europ 151.9

†Actinide Series

90 Th Thorium 232.038	91 Pa Protactinium 231.035	92 U Uranium 238.028	93 Np Neptunium (237)	94 Pu Plutonium (244)	95 Am Amer (243)

Note: Elements with atomic weights in square brackets have no stable isotopes. Different sources lis different atomic weights for elements.

The difference arises from the differing atomic weights of various isotopes. We have tried to list th most stable isotope as per www.science-teachers.com.

11	12	13	14	15	16	17	18
							2 He Helium 4.0026
		5 B Boron 10.811	6 C Carbon 12.0107	7 N Nitrogen 14.007	8 O Oxygen 15.999	9 F Fluorine 18.998	10 Ne Neon 20.179
		13 Al Aluminum 26.9815	14 Si Silicon 28.0855	15 P Phosphorus 30.9737	16 S Sulphur 32.065	17 Cl Chlorine 35.453	18 Ar Argon 39.984
29 Cu Copper 63.546	30 Zn Zinc 65.409	31 Ga Gallium 69.723	32 Ge Germanium 72.59	33 As Arsenic 74.921	34 Se Selenium 78.96	35 Br Bromine 79.904	36 Kr Krypton 83.798
47 Ag Silver 107.868	48 Cd Cadmium 112.411	49 In Indium 114.818	50 Sn Tin 118.710	51 Sb Antimony 121.76	52 Te Tellurium 127.60	53 I Iodine 126.904	54 Xe Xenon 131.293
79 Au Gold 196.966	80 Hg Mercury 200.59	81 Tl Thallium 204.383	82 Pb Lead 207.2	83 Bi Bismuth 208.98	84 Po Polonium (209)	85 At Astatine (210)	86 Rn Radon (222)
111 Rg Roentgenium (272)	112 Cn Copernicium (285)	113 Nh Nihonium (284)	114 Fl Flerovium (289)	115 Mc Moscovium (288)	116 Lv Livermorium (293)	117 Ts Tennessine (294)	118 Og Oganesson (294)

65 Tb Terbium 158.93	66 Dy Dysprosium 162.50	67 Ho Holmium 164.93	68 Er Erbium 167.259	69 Tm Thulium 168.934	70 Yb Ytterbium 173.04	71 Lu Lutetium 174.97
97 Bk Berkelium (247)	98 Cf Californium (251)	99 Es Einsteinium (252)	100 Fm Fermium (257)	101 Md Mendelevium (258)	102 No Nobelium (259)	103 Lr Lawrencium (262)

CHAPTER 28

REACTIVITY SERIES

While studying chemistry, we learn about the reactivity series, which is integral to the subject. This is a series of metals, placed in order of reactivity from highest to lowest. Reactivity can be defined as the tendency of a metal to react with a non-metal. In this series, copper, gold and silver are at the bottom of the hierarchy and, hence, are least reactive. Potassium is at the top of the series and is the most reactive. We need to remember the reactivity series because in a chemical reaction, the more reactive element replaces the less reactive element.

We can remember the sequence of elements in the reactivity series by memorizing a simple sentence, like the one given below, in which the first letter of each word will remind us of the corresponding element in the sequence.

Let's look at this chart for the reactivity of some common metals:

ELEMENT	SYMBOL		MNEMONIC
Potassium	K	**Most reactive**	Please
Sodium	Na		Stop
Calcium	Ca		Calling
Magnesium	Mg		Me
Aluminium	Al		A
Carbon	C		Cute
Zinc	Zn		Zebra
Iron	Fe		Instead
Tin	Sn		Try
Lead	Pb		Learning
Hydrogen	H		How
Copper	Cu		Cops
Silver	Ag		Save
Gold	Au	**Least Reactive**	Golden
Platinum	Pt		Plates

So we can memorize this long and difficult chart using just one simple sentence! Yes, it's that easy. Read this sentence once again and try to recall all the metals by looking at the first letter of each word and remembering the symbol that it denotes.

Please Stop Calling Me A Cute Zebra; Instead Try Learning How Cops Save Golden Plates

There, now you know the reactivity series!

CHAPTER 29

★★★

FORMULAS OF CHEMICAL COMPOUNDS

Chemical formulas are a source of fear for many, especially when the formula does not have any link to its name. For example, the formula for glucose is $C_6H_{12}O_6$. Because of this missing link between the name and formula, students find it difficult to memorize. But once you master the technique to remember formulas, half the battle is won! In this chapter you will learn to memorize the chemical formulas of some important chemical compounds using their common names by associating them through the PNN Method.

Let's begin!

1. **Washing Soda – $Na_2CO_3.10H_2O$**

Formula	PNN
Washing Soda	Washing after drinking soda
Na_2	Nana Patekar (actor)
CO_3 (carbonate)	Car + Bonnet
$10 H_2O$	10 buckets of water

Visualization: After drinking cold soda water on a hot day, Nana Patekar *(Na$_2$)* is washing *(washing soda)* a car bonnet *(CO$_3$)* with 10 buckets of water *(10H$_2$O)*.

2. Borax – $Na_2B_4O_7.10H_2O$

Formula	PNN
Borax	Wild boar + axe
Na_2	Nana Patekar (actor)
B_4	Before
O_7	7 Oxen
$10\ H_2O$	10 buckets of water

Visualization: A wild boar with an axe *(Borax)* is standing with Nana Patekar *(Na₂)* before *(B₄)* 7 oxen *(O₇)* carrying 10 buckets of water *(10H₂O)* on their back.

3. Glucose – $C_6H_{12}O_6$

Formula	PNN
Glucose	Glucose biscuits
C_6	6 Cans
H_{12}	Hide in Den *(phonetic image of 12)*
O_6	6 Oxen

Visualization: Imagine yourself stuffing lots of *glucose* biscuits in 6 cans *(C₆)* and then hiding them in a den *(H₁₂)*. However, when you come back to find them, you see that there are 6 Oxen *(O₆)* there, who are now sitting on each of the cans.

4. Acetic Acid – CH_3COOH

Formula	PNN
Acetic Acid	Ace + Tick – putting a tick on the ace of spades in a set of playing cards
CH_3	Car + 3 Hydrogen bombs
COOH (carboxyl)	Car + Box

Visualization: The ace of spades is marked with a tick *(Acetic)* and placed on a car *(C)*, which carries 3 hydrogen bombs *(H₃)* that are kept in the car box *(carboxyl)*.

5. Aspartame – $C_{14}H_{18}N_2O_5$

Formula	PNN
Aspartame	As + part + time
C_{14}	Car (an image taken for C) + Dr *(phonetic image for 14)*
H_{18}	Hiding a dwarf *(phonetic image for 18)*
N_2	2 Nights
O_5	5 Oxygen cylinders

Visualization: As a part-time job, I drove a car *(C)* belonging to a Dr *(14)*. A dwarf *(18)* was hiding *(H)* in it for 2 nights *(N₂)* with 5 cylinders of oxygen *(O₅)*.

★★★ CONFUSING COMMON NAMES OF ★★★
CHEMICAL COMPOUNDS

Students often get confused by chemical compounds of the same element, and it is a bigger problem if the names of the compounds sound similar. For example, calcium oxide is called quicklime, calcium hydroxide is called slaked lime and calcium carbonate is called limestone. Below is a list of some similar chemical compounds:

S.No.	Chemical Name	Chemical Formula	Common Name
1.	Calcium Oxide	CaO	Quicklime
2.	Calcium Hydroxide	$Ca(OH)_2$	Slaked Lime
3.	Calcium Carbonate	$CaCO_3$	Limestone
4.	Calcium Oxychloride	$CaOCl_2$	Bleaching Powder
5.	Calcium Sulphate Hemihydrate	$CaSO_4.H_2O$	Plaster of Paris

We can use memory clues to memorize the above table by making the following associations:

1. **Calcium Oxide**:
   Chemical formula: CaO
   Common name: Quicklime
   PNN:
   CaO: We can pronounce this as 'cow'
   Quicklime: Drinking lime water quickly
   Visualization: Picture that a **cow** (CaO) is drinking **lime** water very **quickly** (quicklime).

2. **Calcium Hydroxide**:
   Chemical formula: Ca(OH)$_2$
   Common Name: Slaked Lime
   PNN:
   Calcium: Calci (calculator)
   Hydroxide: Hide
   Slaked lime: Lake of lime
   Visualization: A **calci** is **hidden** in the **lake of lime**.

3. **Calcium Carbonate:**
   Chemical Formula: CaCO$_3$
   Common name: Limestone
   PNN:
   Calcium: Calci (calculator)
   Carbonate: Car + bonnet
   Limestone: Name of a stone
   Visualization: Picture that a **calci** kept on a **car bonnet** is as hard as **limestone**.

4. **Calcium Oxychloride**:
   Chemical formula: CaOCl$_2$
   Common name: Bleaching Powder
   PNN:
   CaOCl$_2$: (CaO + Cl$_2$): Cow + 2 Clowns
   Bleaching Powder: Bleach
   Visualization: Imagine a **cow** (CaO) sitting alongside **2 clowns** (Cl$_2$) who have their faces covered in **bleach**.

Now let's say we have to memorize the reaction involved in the production of bleaching powder. The chemical reaction is as follows:

$$Ca(OH)_2 + Cl_2 \longrightarrow CaOCl_2 + H_2O$$

| Slaked Lime | Chlorine | Bleaching Powder | Water |
| (Lake of lime) | (2 Clowns) | (Bleach) | |

188

Visualization:

Picture **2 Clowns** (Cl_2) taking a dip in a **lake of lime**. When they come out, they have **bleach** on their faces, which they wash with **water**.

NOTE: STUDENTS WILL ALREADY KNOW THE FORMULAS FOR SLAKED LIME AND BLEACHING POWDER, AND WE HAVE STUDIED THIS EARLIER, SO WE WILL NOT ELABORATE ON THEIR CHEMICAL NAMES AGAIN. WE CAN USE THEIR COMMON NAMES TO DO THE VISUALIZATION. SO THE VISUALIZATION OF 'LAKE OF LIME' WILL REMIND THE STUDENT OF THE 'CALCI' HIDDEN IN IT, AND FROM THE 'HIDDEN CALCI', THEY WILL BE REMINDED OF CALCIUM HYDROXIDE.

5. **Calcium Sulphate Hemihydrate:**

   Chemical formula: $CaSO_4.H_2O$

   Common name: Plaster of Paris

   PNN:

   $CaSO_4$: Calcium sulphate is Calci + Selfie

   $\frac{1}{2}H_2O$: Half a glass of water

Visualization:

Picture yourself taking a **selfie,** but instead of a phone you're taking it with a **calci** (calculator) and holding **half a glass of water** in your other hand. However, all of a sudden, after clicking the selfie, a 3D image made of **PoP** (Plaster of Paris) comes out.

   After memorizing the chemical compounds and their formulas, complete the following table:

S.No.	Chemical Formula	Common Name
1.	CaO	
2.		Acetic Acid
3.	$Ca(OH)_2$	
4.		Washing Soda
5.		Limestone
6.	$C_{14}H_{18}N_2O_5$	
7.		Bleaching Powder
8.	$CaSO_4.H_2O$	
9.		Glucose
10.	$Na_2B_4O_7.10\,H_2O$	

Learning chemical formulas can be very interesting. Have you ever had this much fun before while learning formulas and the common names of compounds? Memory techniques make everything easy, so go ahead and use these techniques to memorize many more formulas with ease.

CHAPTER 30

CHEMICAL REACTIONS

Chemical nomenclatures (or chemical names) are one of the first things we learn in chemistry. These names are universally used, and students of chemistry can easily remember them without confusion. For example, it's easy to remember that the chemical name of NaOH is sodium hydroxide; however, common names can create a lot of confusion: is NaOH caustic soda, baking soda or washing soda? It is important to note that all these compounds have their different chemical formulas, dissimilar processes of manufacturing and varied uses. So the first step in giving the right answer is recalling the varied properties and remembering the right name of the compounds involved.

We already know that the brain stores information in the form of images, so we can picture these compounds to remove any confusion. Let's look at the examples below:

1. Caustic Soda

The common name of sodium hydroxide (NaOH) is caustic soda. Using the PNN Method, we derive the associations:

NaOH (Na–O–H): This can be pronounced 'now'.
Caustic Soda: Cast + Soda

Visualization:

Right **now** (NaOH) the whole **cast** (caustic) of the film is drinking **soda** water after a long day of shooting.

The reaction involved in the manufacture of caustic soda is shown below:

NaOH is produced when electricity is passed through an aqua solution of sodium chloride, called brine. The other products formed are chlorine and hydrogen gas. Here's the chemical equation for the same:

$$2NaCl + 2H_2O \xrightarrow{\text{Electric Current}} 2NaOH + Cl_2 + H_2$$

| Sodium Chloride | Water | | Caustic Soda | Chlorine gas | Hydrogen gas |

Brine

Visualization to memorize reaction:

Visualize that **now** (NaOH) an electric current is being passed through a solution of **sodium chloride** (NaCl) and **water** (H_2O). This solution is good for the **brain** (brine).

NOTE: BYPRODUCTS OF SODIUM HYDROXIDE—CHLORINE AND HYDROGEN GAS—CAN EASILY BE REMEMBERED, AS CHEMISTRY STUDENTS LEARN HOW TO BALANCE THE EQUATION.

2. Baking Soda

Sodium hydrogen carbonate ($NaHCO_3$) is called baking soda. It is commonly used in the kitchen to make crispy snacks and in baking; it is a major component of baking powder. It is produced using sodium chloride, which acts as one of the raw materials.

Using the PNN Method, we derive the associations:

Baking Soda: Baking cake with soda
Sodium Hydrogen Carbonate: Soda + hide + car bonnet

Visualization:

Picture that your friend wants to **bake a cake with soda**; however, there isn't any at home. So he takes the **soda** bottle **hidden** in the **car bonnet** to add to his cake.

The reaction involved in the manufacture of baking soda is shown below:

$$NaCl + H_2O + CO_2 + NH_3 \longrightarrow NaHCO_3 + NH_4Cl$$

| Brine | Carbon Dioxide | Ammonia | | Baking Soda | Ammonium Chloride |

We can visualize the compounds involved in the reaction by using the PNN Method as shown below:

NaCl: Common salt
H₂O: Water
Brine: Brain
Carbon Dioxide: Visualize it as smoke, as it causes pollution
Ammonia: Pneumonia
Baking Soda: Baking cake with soda

Visualization:
Imagine that a boy was told that drinking a solution of **common salt** ($NaCl$) dissolved in **water** (H_2O) was good for the **brain** (Brine). However, some **smoke** (CO_2) that was being emitted from the environment spoiled it, and he got **pneumonia** (NH_3).

To get well, he **baked a cake with soda** (baking soda) and felt much better.

What did you think of these exercises? Are they not easier to remember now through these visualizations? Using memory techniques works because it seems like you are watching a movie while learning chemistry! It's a whole lot of fun while you learn. Try more equations by applying all the methods that you have learnt so far.

★★★

CHAPTER 31

CLEARING CONFUSION

Many times we come across information that seems easy to understand at first but then leads to confusion. In this chapter we are going to look into this and learn how to use memory techniques to make associations that will enable us to eliminate confusion and recall information or answers without any mistakes.

Example 1:
Difference between oxidation and reduction reactions.
Oxidation – When a reactant loses one or more electrons during a chemical reaction
Reduction – When a reactant gains electrons during the reaction

Confusion arises when you try to remember which case has a loss of electrons and which one has a gain of electrons.

The Memory Solution
We can memorize it by simply using the acronym –
OIL RIG
OIL: **O**xidation **I**nvolves **L**oss (of electrons)
RIG: **R**eduction **I**nvolves **G**ain (of electrons)

Example 2:

Cations and Anions

Cations: They are positively charged ions.

Anions: They are negatively charged ions.

The Memory Solution:

We can use the PNN Method for *anions* and visualize them as **onions**.

Visualize that cutting onions brings tears to your eyes. So, onions (anions) are negatively charged. This way you'll know cations are positively charged ions.

Example 3:

Isotopes and Isobars

Isotopes: They are atoms of the same element having the same atomic number but different mass number.

Isobars: They are atoms of different elements with different atomic numbers but the same mass number.

It is confusing to remember which case has a mass number that is different and which case has elements that are different.

The Memory Solution:

We can make use of the PNN Method and some other associations to memorize the difference.

Using the PNN Method, we can visualize *isotopes* as a number of **tops** (or **earrings**) for women, all made from the same material, say silver (or another element), but are of different sizes (different masses).

Visualize *isobars* as **ice-cream bars**. Different bars (different elements), like a mango bar, choco bar and strawberry bar, have different tastes but are packed or made to be the same size (same mass).

Follow these techniques to make your own associations for similar information that seems confusing to you. It will bring clarity and will make it easy to recall information.

VI. PHYSICS

CHAPTER 32

MEASURING INSTRUMENTS

Measurement is the basic requirement of almost every science experiment, be it studying about units and dimensions of a body or going through complex theories of electricity and magnetism. You need to know about different measuring instruments used to measure different quantities such as temperature, speed and pressure. However, remembering the names of all the instruments can be tricky. Let's see how you can memorize the names of the various instruments using memory techniques.

S. No.	INSTRUMENT	USED TO MEASURE
1.	Rain gauge	Rainfall
2.	Speedometer	Speed of a vehicle
3.	Magnetometer	Magnetism
4.	Thermometer	Temperature
5.	Barometer	Atmospheric pressure
6.	Bolometer	Electromagnetic radiations
7.	Photometer	Intensity of light
8.	Galvanometer	Small electric currents
9.	Pyrometer	High temperature of a surface
10.	Sphygmomanometer	Blood pressure
11.	Anemometer	Speed of wind
12.	Salinometer	Amount of salt in a liquid

As you can see, the names of some instruments suggest their use. Hence, recalling these are not difficult. For example, you can deduce quite easily that a rain gauge is used to measure rainfall, a speedometer is used to measure the speed of a vehicle and a magnetometer is used to measure magnetism. However, the same cannot be said for other instruments, as some of the words are difficult to understand.

So, let's memorize all of these with the help of the PNN Method.

For example:

Galvanometer measures small electric currents
Galvanometer: Gal + van

MEASURING INSTRUMENTS

Visualization: A girl (*gal*) is sitting in her favourite *van*. She is sending *electric currents* to whoever touches her van.

Now, let's look at the table below for the other measuring instruments:

S. No.	Instrument	PNN	Used to measure	Visualization
1.	Barometer	Bar	Atmospheric pressure	In this **bar**, soda water comes out of the bottle with high **pressure**.
2.	Bolometer	Polo (a game)	Electromagnetic radiation	To be safe from the effect of **electromagnetic radiation**s, the boy went out to play **polo**.
3.	Photometer	Photo	Light intensity	I clicked a **photo** to **light** up the dark room.
4.	Pyrometer	Pyre	High temperature of a surface	The **surface temperature** of the **pyre** is too high, so you cannot touch it.
5.	Sphygmo-manometer	Pig + Mom + no	Blood pressure	Imagine that you see a family of pigs in the countryside, and the **pig**'s **mom** is saying **no** to the doctor who is trying to measure her **blood pressure**.

S. No.	Instrument	PNN	Used to measure	Visualization
6.	Anemometer	A neem (tree)	Speed of wind	A big **neem** tree is uprooted by high-**speed winds**.
7.	Salinometer	Sail + no	Amount of salt in liquid	Your friend said **no** to **sailing** in a boat, because the **amount of salt in the sea** was too high.

You may note that it is not necessary to associate 'meter' every time, as it is common to all.

You may memorize similar information, like the different kinds of phobias (acrophobia or cynophobia, for example), or the names of different subjects of study (like geology, agrology, nephrology or oology) using memory techniques. Forming nicknames using the PNN Method and then visualizing these will make this a fun but creative process.

CHAPTER 33

UNITS OF MEASUREMENTS

In order to understand the metric system (the decimal system of weights and measurements), students must **memorize** the base *units* for each type of measurement. A base unit is the fundamental unit in a system of measurement, like meter or kilogramme. By using memory techniques, students can easily learn the units of measurement with clarity. Let's learn it with some examples.

QUANTITY TO BE MEASURED	UNIT
Inductance	*Henry*
Electrical resistance	*Ohm*
Quantity of electricity	*Coulomb*
Electric conductance	*Siemens*
Magnetic induction	*Tesla*
Plane angle	*Radian*
Current	*Ampere*
Power	*Watt*
Energy	*Joule*
Force	*Newton*
Pressure	*Pascal*
Temperature	*Kelvin*
Frequency	*Hertz*
Luminous intensity	*Candela*
Potential difference	*Volt*

In the table, many quantities (like power, energy, force and pressure) seem alike, but they all are different and have different units of measurement. So at times it's very confusing to learn them. But by using memory techniques, we will be able to memorize the table. We will now make PNNs for the quantities to be measured along with their respective units, and then visualize the association between them.

1. **Inductance – Henry**

   Inductance: Induction Cooker (PNN)

   Henri: Hen (PNN)

   Visualization: The **hen** is cooking food on an **induction** cooker.

2. **Electrical resistance – Ohm**

   Electrical resistance: Resist electricity (PNN)

   Ohm: Om (PNN)

   Visualization: Someone is telling you that if you chant 'om' for a long time, you can develop the power to **resist electricity**.

3. **Quantity of electricity – Coulomb**

   Coulomb: Column (PNN)

   Visualization: To find the **quantity of electricity**, count the number of **columns** in the building structure.

4. **Electric conductance – Siemens**
   Electric conductance: Electric bus conductor (PNN)
   Siemens: See men (PNN)
   Visualization: There is an **electric bus conductor** who is happy to **see** that all the **men** are sitting in the bus and following the safety rules.

5. **Magnetic induction – Tesla**
   Magnetic induction: Magnet industry (PNN)
   Tesla: Test (PNN)
   Visualization: You are being asked to **test magnets in the industry**.

6. **Plane angle – Radian**
   Plane angle: Airplane + anger (PNN)
   Radian: Red + ions (PNN)
   Visualization: An **angry airplane** is emitting **red ions** in the sky.

7. **Current – Ampere**
   Current: Current
   Ampere: Empire (PNN)
   Visualization: You ask a prince, 'What is your **current** position in the **empire**?'

8. **Power – Watt**
   Power: Powerful person (PNN)
   Watt: What (PNN)
   Visualization: You see an important person at a party and think, '**What** a **powerful** person he is!'

9. Energy – Joule

Energy: Energetic (PNN)

Joule: Jewel (PNN)

Visualization: Think of a scenario in which all **energetic** people are given **jewels**.

10. Force – Newton

Force: Air force (PNN)

Newton: Newton (PNN)

Visualization: Imagine seeing Isaac **Newton** applying to the Indian **Air Force**.

11. Pressure – Pascal

Pressure: Pressure cooker (PNN)

Pascal: Pass + call (PNN)

Visualization: Think of a huge **pressure** cooker **call**ing you to let him **pass** by you.

12. Temperature – Kelvin

Temperature: Temperature

Kelvin: Kelvinator refrigerator (PNN)

Visualization: The **Kelvinator** refrigerator keeps the **temperature** cool.

13. Frequency – Hertz

Frequency: Frequently (PNN)

Hertz: Hearts (PNN)

Visualization: Think of a **heart** beating fast and **frequently.**

14. Luminous intensity – Candela

Luminous intensity: Light intensity (PNN)

Candela: Candle (PNN)

Visualization: You've lit a candle in a dark room, and the **candle light** is spreading all around **intensely**.

15. Potential difference – Volt

Potential difference: Difference in potential

Volt: Voltas (PNN)

Visualization: You are at a store selecting a refrigerator, and the salesman tells you, 'There is a lot of **difference in potential** between both these **Voltas** refrigerators.'

Once you have made the associations in your mind, try to see if you are able to recall the units correctly. You will be surprised with the results!

CHAPTER 34

★★★

UNIVERSAL CONSTANTS

In physics, students use various constants while doing numerical work. For this, they have to memorize the values of such constants, which consist of large numbers that can be quite confusing at times. To memorize such constants, we make use of the PNN Method and the Phonetic Method along with the Chain Method.

1. **1 Light Year = 9.46×10^{12} km**

    Light year: Can be visualized as light received for one whole year
    9.46: 946 (brg) – bridge. Here, the *d is silent (Phonetic Method)*
    12: den *(Phonetic Method)*

Visualization: You are walking on a bridge *(946) that receives light* for one whole year to reach the valley of 10 secret dens (10^{12}).

2. **Mass of the Moon = 7.34×10^{22}**

    7.34: 734 (kmr) - kamera *(Phonetic Method)*
    22: nun *(Phonetic Method)*

Visualization: A team of 10 nuns (10^{22}) is going to the *moon* to check its *mass* with a special camera (*kamera 734*).

3. Gravitational constant G = 6.67 × 10^{-11} *Nm² / kg²*

G: Gravitation of Earth
6.67: Judge + Key *(Phonetic Method)*
11* : dad *(Phonetic Method)*

Visualization: Due to the *constant gravitational* pull of *Earth*, the special judge key (*6.67*) (a key that a judge possesses), falls on the Earth and 10 dads (*10^{-11}*) are fighting (–) to grab it.

4. Mass of Neutron = 1.67 × 10^{-27} kg

Neutron: New train *(PNN Method)*
1.67: Dash key *(Phonetic Method)*
10: hen *(Rhyme Method)*
−27*: broken + neck *(Phonetic Method)*

Visualization: The mass of a *new train* can be calculated by pressing the dash key *(1.67)* on the keyboard. The train is so light that even a hen *(10)* can lift it on its broken neck *(−27)*.

5. Charge on One Electron = −1.6 × 10^{-19} C

Electron: Electral powder (Oral Rehydration Salt or ORS)
−1.6*: hollow + dish *(Phonetic Method)*
−19*: tap *(Phonetic Method)* without water
C: charge

Visualization: You put *Electral powder* in a hollow dish *(–1.6)* to dissolve it in water. You tried to use 10 taps, but all of them were dry and there was no water *(–10⁻¹⁹)*. So you took it in the powder form to charge (C) yourself.

* Wherever there is a negative sign (–) in the number, the phonetic image we have made is one that is a little negative (undesirable). For example, the phonetic code for 27 is neck but since it was –27, we have visualized it as a broken neck. Similarly, in case of 19, the phonetic image is a tap, but we have shown it as a tap without water to represent –19. You may create some other associations of your choice.

By now you must be familiar with the Phonetic Method of coding numbers to memorize numerical constants or other information including numbers. So, explore your own imagination and creativity by memorizing similar information to master the technique.

Visualization: You put *Electral powder* in a hollow dish *(–1.6)* to dissolve it in water. You tried to use 10 taps, but all of them were dry and there was no water *(–10⁻¹⁹)*. So you took it in the powder form to charge (C) yourself.

CHAPTER 35

★★★

PHYSICS FORMULAS

Learning physics involves understanding, deriving and memorizing formulas, which can seem problematic for students given the many tables, formulas, charts and facts they need to remember. But knowing formulas by heart can be made easy. Let's learn some in this chapter by making creative visualizations.

Formula 1: In all spherical mirrors the relation between the object's distance, image's distance and the focal length of the mirror can be given as follows:

Mirror Formula: $\dfrac{1}{v} + \dfrac{1}{u} = \dfrac{1}{f}$

where, v = image distance from pole of mirror
u = object distance from pole of mirror
f = focal length

Formula 2:
In case of all spherical lenses, the relation between the above three can be given as follows:

$$\frac{1}{v} - \frac{1}{u} = \frac{1}{f}$$

The confusion lies in the sign +/− involved in the formulas and also in memorizing the formulas.

The Memory Solution:

For the mirror formula: Visualize that you are standing in front of a mirror and saying to your image:

We (**v**) and (**+**) You (**u**) are Forever (**f**)

For the lens formula: Visualize that you are wearing spectacles (lens) and you are suggesting to yourself that you will get rid of these spectacles soon by saying:

We (**v**) are not (**−**) with You (**u**) Forever (**f**)

Formula 3:

In case of horizontal motion, to find the distance travelled by a body when its initial velocity, acceleration and time taken are given, we use the Distance–Acceleration equation, which is given as:

$$s = ut + \frac{1}{2}at^2$$

where s = displacement covered
u = initial velocity
t = time taken
a = acceleration of the body

The Memory Solution:

Imagine that the body that is moving is of a small rabbit.

Visualize that the rabbit is sitting under a tree and chewing half an apple with 2 of its front teeth.

sitting	under	tree	and	eating half	apple	with 2 front teeth
s =	u	t	+	$\frac{1}{2}$	a	t^2

Formula 4:

In case of a simple pendulum, when a bob is suspended to a string, the time period of one oscillation is given by the formula:

$$\text{Time period} = T = 2\pi\sqrt{\frac{l}{g}}$$

Where T = time period

l = length of the string of pendulum

g = acceleration due to gravity

The Memory Solution:

Here we will make associations for the symbols used in the formula with some images, as shown below:

T	time taken
2π	2 pies
$\sqrt{}$	square root can be visualized as going inside a room
l	light of God
g	girl

Visualization: Imagine that you take very little time to eat two pies and then you go inside a room in which a girl is sitting under the divine light of God.

The examples given here show how to memorize tricky information using creative visualizations. It is better to use your own creativity, something that you can connect to, to make your own visualizations so that it is embedded in your mind. That way, you can recall with ease.

VII. MATHEMATICS

CHAPTER 36

THE TIMES TABLES

During our numerous training sessions with students and teachers, we found that very few students remember the times tables in mathematics thoroughly. This results in their output constantly being affected by their inability to multiply and divide quickly. Here, we are talking about students not just at the primary level but also those at the higher secondary level.

The multiplication tables are always thought to be something that should be memorized by heart, by rote memorization, through chanting or through singing songs. But it has been observed that most students, especially those at the primary level, need to recite or mentally recall the *whole* table if asked to recall, say, 6 × 7. Secondly, rote learning leads to confusion. If a child memorizes a wrong value once, then it may remain embedded in their memory forever.

As we have discovered in the previous chapters, our brain remembers pictures more easily than numbers. We will try to make learning the multiplication tables easier by teaching you some memory solutions in the form of images that are hilarious in nature. These will help you register the facts easily, quickly and correctly.

Using these memory techniques, we created a **Guinness World Record** in 2012 for teaching *the largest maths class*, involving 2312 students, where we taught them the techniques to memorize the tables till 99. In this book, we have discussed visualizations for a few confusing numbers for the tables till 9. However, to know more about the technique of **learning the times tables from 12 to 99,** you can refer to *How to Be a Mathemagician* (Penguin Random House, 2017).

In this chapter, we will make use of the Rhyme Method (learnt in Chapter 6) to convert the factors and multiples in the multiplication tables into creative images. We have already learnt the rhyming images for the numbers one to twelve, which we will use for the factors. For the multiples, we can make new images that match their rhyming sound.

RHYME METHOD

1		2	
ONE	SUN	**TWO**	SHOE
3		4	
THREE	TREE	**FOUR**	DOOR
5		6	
FIVE	HIVE	**SIX**	STICKS

7 **SEVEN**	 LEMON	8 **EIGHT**	 PLATE
9 **NINE**	 LINE	10 **TEN**	 HEN
11 **ELEVEN**	 HEAVEN	12 **TWELVE**	 SHELF

Some Confusing Facts

Most of the time students are easily able to memorize the tables up to 5; even if they are not able to recall it immediately, they work out the tables through simple repeated addition. But as they progress to the higher tables, many students are not comfortable in repeatedly adding bigger numbers like 6, 7 or 8. Memorizing big numbers also becomes difficult for many. It has been observed that students make more mistakes in the tables of 6, 7 and 8.

While interacting with students, we zeroed in on some particular multiplications in which most students get confused, though these may differ from child to child.

6 × 3	=	18
6 × 7	=	42
6 × 9	=	54
7 × 3	=	21
7 × 7	=	49
7 × 8	=	56
8 × 3	=	24
8 × 8	=	64

Let's make some rhyming images for the multiples we have to memorize:

Multiples	Rhyming Image
18	Aching
42	Naughty Shoe
21	Aunty One
49	Fort Shine
56	Fishing Sticks*
24	Plenty Doors
64	Sticky Floor
54	Lifting Door

*We have taken 56 as 'Fishing Sticks' as the rhyming sound of 56 matches it. Although they are technically called fishing rods, for visualization purposes we can use the term fishing sticks.

You can have your own rhyming images for the above multiples. Go through these and repeat the images in your mind two to three times before going ahead with the associations.

Now we will make the associations between our confusing facts and the rhyming images to memorize them.

Confusing Fact 1:

$$6 \times 3 = 18$$

Sticks × Tree = Aching

Visualization: Visualize that **sticks** (6) are falling from a **tree** (3), and as you gather all those sticks, your hands start **aching** (18).

Confusing Fact 2:

$$6 \times 7 = 42$$

Sticks × Lemon = Naughty Shoe

Visualization: Imagine that a shoe has come to life. This **naughty shoe** (42) is playing with **sticks** (6) and **lemons** (7). It is throwing lemons all over the house and hitting them with the sticks as it walks.

Confusing Fact 3:

$$6 \times 9 = 54$$

Sticks × Line = Lifting Door

Visualization: Visualize a situation in which people are standing in a long **line** (9) with **sticks** (6) in their hands, with which they are **lifting** a **door** (54).

Confusing Fact 4:

$$7 \times 3 = 21$$

Lemon × Tree = Aunty One

Visualization: Imagine that your favourite aunty, whom you lovingly call **Aunty One** (21), is decorating a **tree** (3) with **lemons** (7), making a criss-cross design.

Confusing Fact 5:

$$7 \times 7 = 49$$

Lemon × Lemon = **Fort Shine**

Visualization: Visualize that you're scrubbing a fort vigorously with two **lemons** (7×7), using both your hands. Soon the **fort** starts **shining** (49) beautifully.

Confusing Fact 6:

$$7 \times 8 = 56$$

Lemon × Plate = Fishing Sticks

Visualization: Imagine that a fisherman is preparing for his fishing trip by keeping **lemons** (7) on a large **plate** (8). He will later use these lemons as bait by attaching them to his **fishing sticks** (56).

Confusing Fact 7:

$$8 \times 3 = 24$$

Plate × Tree = Plenty Doors

Visualization: Picture that on a huge **plate** (8), a magical **tree** (3) has been planted, which grows to have **plenty** of **doors** (24) on it.

Confusing Fact 8:

$$8 \times 8 = 64$$

Plate × Plate = Sticky Floor

Visualization: Visualize a hilarious scenario where one animated **plate** (8) is trying to climb on top of another **plate** (8) as they both try to avoid the **sticky floor** (64).

Sometimes you may take a little time to learn these associations, but once you practise them thoroughly, these will be embedded in your memory forever.

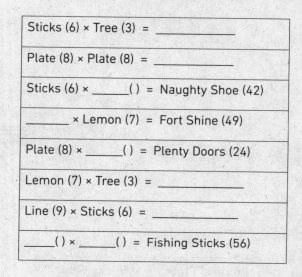

Sticks (6) × Tree (3) = _____
Plate (8) × Plate (8) = _____
Sticks (6) × _____( ) = Naughty Shoe (42)
_____ × Lemon (7) = Fort Shine (49)
Plate (8) × _____( ) = Plenty Doors (24)
Lemon (7) × Tree (3) = _____
Line (9) × Sticks (6) = _____
_____( ) × _____( ) = Fishing Sticks (56)

You have learnt the associations for eight confusing facts. However, in reality you have memorized sixteen facts from the times tables, as multiplication is commutative. Isn't that fascinating? For example, whenever you have to answer *6 × 7 or 7 × 6*, you will be reminded of sticks and lemons in either case; and if you try to recall the visualization or question what you were doing with sticks and lemons, you will automatically be reminded of a naughty shoe, which is 42.

You can make similar visualizations for other multiplication tables, especially the ones you find difficult or confusing.

CHAPTER 37

★ ★ ★

TRIGONOMETRY-I

There's one subject that gives everyone sweaty palms, and that's mathematics. One topic in particular is feared by most—trigonometry. It is not only a dreaded subject but also a phobia for many students, as everyone seems to be scared of numbers. There are also confusing formulas, which have to be memorized. Hence, many find it hard; firstly, there are just too many formulas, and secondly, they are very much alike. So in this chapter we will take on this much-feared subject and apply some memory clues to memorize these formulas. These can then be learnt easily and will remain in your memory forever.

To memorize the **trigonometry ratios**, you just need to memorize an acrostic. An acrostic is a form of mnemonic, in which the first letter of each word or term is used to form some new words that then make a meaningful sentence or phrase.

Here's our acrostic:

Some people have curly brown hair turned permanently black.
Yes, that's all you need to know to memorize the trigonometry ratios. So let's look at the ratio:

Some People Have   *Curly Brown Hair*   *Turned Permanently Black*

$$S = \frac{P}{H} \qquad C = \frac{B}{H} \qquad T = \frac{P}{B}$$

$$\mathbf{S}in = \frac{\mathbf{P}erpendicular}{\mathbf{H}ypotenuse} \qquad \mathbf{C}os = \frac{\mathbf{B}ase}{\mathbf{H}ypotenuse}$$

$$\mathbf{T}an = \frac{\mathbf{P}erpendicular}{\mathbf{B}ase}$$

Now let's study the other three ratios: *Cosec, Sec* and *Cot.* For these, just remember the following:

Cosec is the reciprocal of Sin, or $\mathbf{Cosec} = \dfrac{1}{\mathrm{Sin}} = \dfrac{H}{P}$

Sec is the reciprocal of Cos, or $\mathbf{Sec} = \dfrac{1}{\mathrm{Cos}} = \dfrac{H}{B}$

Cot is the reciprocal of Tan, or $\mathbf{Cot} = \dfrac{1}{\mathrm{Tan}} = \dfrac{B}{P}$

There's another hilarious method of learning these formulas:

Pandit	**B**adri	**P**rasad	$\dfrac{P}{H}$	$\dfrac{B}{H}$	$\dfrac{P}{B}$
Har	**H**ar	**B**ole	=	=	=
Sona	**C**handi	**T**ole	Sin	Cos	Tan

232

★★★ SUM AND DIFFERENCE FORMULAS ★★★

Let's say we have to memorize the following four trigonometry formulas:

1. $\sin(A+B) = \sin A \cos B + \cos A \sin B$
2. $\sin(A-B) = \sin A \cos B - \cos A \sin B$
3. $\cos(A+B) = \cos A \cos B - \sin A \sin B$
4. $\cos(A-B) = \cos A \cos B + \sin A \sin B$

The above formulas seem very confusing as sine and cosine ratios are appearing many times in all of them. We know that the mind understands the language of images, so we will learn these formulas by visualizing the sine and cosine ratios as some character, and then making associations for the confusing parts.

Let's assume that sine and cosine are individuals.

Consider *sine* as a good character and *cosine* as a bad character, both with some specific traits:

S. NO.	SINE	COSINE
1.	Good	Bad
2.	Gives equal opportunities	Discriminates
3.	Does what he is told	Always does the opposite of what he is told
4.	Shares equally	Wants more for himself

Formula 1:

$$\sin(A+B) = \underbrace{\sin A \cos B}_{1st\ part} + \underbrace{\cos A \sin B}_{2nd\ part}$$

The Memory Clue:

On the left-hand side of the formula is sin *(A + B)*, which suggests that it is the formula of sine. Since we have assumed *sine* is a person with *good* character, who gives equal opportunities to all, we assume he gives equal opportunities to himself as well as to the other person—cosine.

Therefore in the first part, sine leads (as he's good) followed by cosine (who is bad), i.e., sin*A*cos*B*.

In the second part, sine gives an equal opportunity to cosine, so cosine leads, followed by sine, i.e., cos*A*sin*B*.

$$\therefore \ \sin(A+B) = \sin A \cos B + \cos A \sin B$$

Since in (A + B) there is the positive sign, and *sine* does as told (being a person of good character), it maintains '+' on the other side as well.

Formula 2:

$$\sin(A-B) = \underbrace{\sin A \cos B}_{1st\ part} - \underbrace{\cos A \sin B}_{2nd\ part}$$

The Memory Clue:

The technique that we will use will follow the same rule, so the method is going to be the same as before.

Since there is a negative sign on the left-hand side (LHS), we assume that *sine* maintains it on the right-hand side (RHS) as well.

$$\therefore \ \sin(A-B) = \sin A \cos B - \cos A \sin B$$

Formula 3:

$$\cos(A+B) = \underbrace{\cos A \cos B}_{1st\ part} - \underbrace{\sin A \sin B}_{2nd\ part}$$

The Memory Clue:

We know that cosine or sine can take only two positions, and since this is a *cosine* formula and we know that *he is a bad person* who prioritizes only himself, he takes both the position in the first part, i.e., cos$A$cos$B$ and then gives both the remaining positions of the second part to sine, i.e., sin$A$sin$B$.

$$\therefore \cos(A+B) = \cos A \cos B - \sin A \sin B$$

Since cosine always does the opposite, the positive (+) sign on the LHS changes to the negative (−) sign on the RHS.

Formula 4:

$$\cos(A-B) = \underbrace{\cos A \cos B}_{1st\ part} + \underbrace{\sin A \sin B}_{2nd\ part}$$

The Memory Clue:

The trigonometric ratios remain the same in this formula except for the sign involved in the middle. To memorize this, we can assume as before that cosine takes both positions in the first part and gives both positions in the second part to sine. Since there is the negative (−) sign on the LHS, it changes to the positive (+) sign on the RHS, as cosine always does the opposite.

The formulas cannot be visualized word for word, as that will make it a very long visualization. So we make the associations for only the confusing parts. We will see some more formulas like this in the next chapter.

★★★

CHAPTER 38

⭐⭐⭐

TRIGONOMETRY-2

In this chapter we will continue to learn some more formulas used in trigonometry with the help of the assumed characteristics of **sine** and **cosine**, as explained in the previous chapter.

⭐⭐⭐ PART 1: SUM AND DIFFERENCE ⭐⭐⭐ TO PRODUCT FORMULAS

Let's memorize the following four trigonometry formulas now:

1) $\sin C + \sin D = 2\sin\left(\dfrac{C+D}{2}\right)\cos\left(\dfrac{C-D}{2}\right)$

2) $\cos C + \cos D = 2\cos\left(\dfrac{C+D}{2}\right)\cos\left(\dfrac{C-D}{2}\right)$

3) $\sin C - \sin D = 2\cos\left(\dfrac{C+D}{2}\right)\sin\left(\dfrac{C-D}{2}\right)$

4) $\cos C - \cos D = -2\sin\left(\dfrac{C+D}{2}\right)\sin\left(\dfrac{C-D}{2}\right)$

In all four formulas, you can observe that on the right-hand-side (RHS) a few things are the same, i.e., the common parts are: the numeral **2** and **angles** $\left[\left(\dfrac{C+D}{2}\right) and \left(\dfrac{C-D}{2}\right)\right]$, as shown below:

$$RHS: 2 \underline{\hspace{1.5cm}} \left(\dfrac{C+D}{2}\right) \underline{\hspace{1.5cm}} \left(\dfrac{C-D}{2}\right)$$

Trigonometric ratios are different here. The arrow above points to the two blanks spaces where the trigonometric ratios are to be inserted. The numeral 2 and the angles remain the same in all formulas of this type; only the ratio changes. So we need to make clues for only the *trigonometric ratios*. In this chapter we will use the same characteristics of sine and cosine as visualized in the previous chapter to memorize this.

The Memory Clues:

Formula 1:

$$\sin C + \sin D = 2 \sin\left(\dfrac{C+D}{2}\right)\cos\left(\dfrac{C-D}{2}\right)$$

We have assumed *sine* has *good* character and shares equally everything with *cosine*. Since it is a **sine formula**, it leads, taking the first position itself and giving the second position to cosine.

Formula 2:

$$\cos C + \cos D = 2 \cos\left(\dfrac{C+D}{2}\right)\cos\left(\dfrac{C-D}{2}\right)$$

Since *cosine is bad* and selfish, it keeps both positions to itself.

Formula 3:

$$\sin C - \sin D = 2\cos\left(\frac{C+D}{2}\right)\sin\left(\frac{C-D}{2}\right)$$

In this formula, the negative (–) sign can be thought of as some kind of *loss*. As *sine* suffers a loss, *cosine* takes advantage and takes the lead. Thus, *sine* has to take the second position.

Formula 4:

$$\cos C - \cos D = -2\sin\left(\frac{C+D}{2}\right)\sin\left(\frac{C-D}{2}\right)$$

As there is a minus (–) sign between the cosines, we can assume the minus sign to be a loss to cosine this time. After suffering a loss, *cosine* regrets its bad behaviour. It wants to apologize to *sine*, so it gives away both parts to *sine*, but it also transfers the losses to sine, so there is a negative (–) sign on the RHS.

★★★ PART 2: PRODUCT TO SUM AND ★★★ DIFFERENCE FORMULAS

Let's say we have to memorize the four following trigonometry formulas:

1) $2\sin A\cos B = \sin(A+B) + \sin(A-B)$

2) $2\cos A\cos B = \cos(A+B) + \cos(A-B)$

3) $2\cos A\sin B = \sin(A+B) - \sin(A-B)$

4) $2\sin A\sin B = \cos(A+B) - \cos(A-B)$

In all the above four formulas, you can observe that the angles are the same on the RHS, i.e.,

$$RHS: \underline{\qquad} (A+B) \pm \underline{\qquad}(A-B)$$

So, we need to make clues for the *trigonometric ratios* and signs in the middle.

If you have understood the earlier section, then you will find this very easy, as the situation is just reversed in this case.

The Memory Clues:

Formula 1:

$$2\sin A\cos B = \sin(A+B) + \sin(A-B)$$

Since the product on the left-hand-side (LHS) is of *sine* and *cosine* both, on the RHS it should be **sine** formulas, as *sine* gives equal opportunities to both, and shares equally. Also, as *sine* is leading the LHS, the sign in the middle of the RHS must be positive (+), as you have seen in the previous chapter.

Formula 2:

$$2\cos A\cos B = \cos(A + B) + \cos(A - B)$$

Since the product on the LHS is of *cosine* only, the ratios on the RHS must be *cosine*. As *cosine is bad* and selfish, it takes both positions itself and does not give opportunities to others.

Formula 3:

$$2\cos A\sin B = \sin(A + B) - \sin(A - B)$$

Since the product on the LHS is of both *cosine* and *sine*, on the RHS it should be **sine** formula, as *sine* gives equal opportunities to both and shares equally. But as *cosine* is leading the LHS, cosine is taking preference over *sine*, which can happen when *sine* suffers a loss (or –). So the sign in the middle of the RHS must be negative (–).

Formula 4:

$$2\sin A\sin B = \cos(A + B) - \cos(A - B)$$

This time both ratios on the LHS are of *sine*, which is possible only when *cosine* offers a chance to *sine* to take both the positions. Therefore, it must be the formula of *cosine* on the RHS, and it must have suffered losses. Because only then does it give its position to *sine*. Thus, on the RHS, the sign in the middle should be negative (–) indicating the *loss to cosine*.

Now practise these formulas by repeating the associations in your mind and then writing them down. You may then experiment with other trigonometry formulas.

VIII. BUSINESS STUDIES

CHAPTER 39

MERITS AND DEMERITS OF PARTNERSHIP

A very interesting way to learn long answers is to associate them with real-life people and visualize them in real-life situations. This is particularly useful in subjects like business studies, social studies and political science—subjects that deal with people and our day-to-day lives. Let's understand this by applying the following business studies answer to a similar kind of situation that has real-life characters.

Q: Why is partnership considered by some to be a relatively unpopular form of business ownership? Explain the merits and limitations of partnership.

Ans.: Merits:

(i) **Ease of formation and closure:**
A partnership can be formed easily by putting an agreement between the prospective partners into place whereby they agree to carry out the business of the firm and share the risks. There is no compulsion with respect to registration, and the closure of the firm is also an easy task.

(ii) **Balanced decision-making:**
The partners can oversee different functions according to their areas of expertise. As an individual is not forced to

handle different activities, this not only reduces the burden of work but also leads to fewer errors in judgement. As a result, decisions are likely to be more balanced.

(iii) More funds:

In a partnership, the capital is contributed by a number of partners. This makes it possible to raise larger amounts of funds as compared to being the sole proprietor, and further undertake additional operations when needed.

(iv) Sharing of risks:

The risks involved in running a partnership firm are shared by all the partners. This reduces anxiety, burden and stress on individual partners.

(v) Secrecy:

A partnership firm is not legally required to publish its accounts and submit its reports. Hence, it is able to maintain confidentiality of information relating to its operations.

Limitations:

(i) Unlimited liability:

Partners are liable to repay debts, even if it comes from their personal resources, in case the business assets are not sufficient to meet its debts. The liability of partners is both joint and several, which may prove to be a drawback for those partners who have greater personal wealth. They will have to pay the entire debt in case the other partners are unable to do so.

(ii) Limited resources:

There is a restriction on the number of partners, so contribution in terms of capital investment is usually not sufficient to support a large-scale business operation. As a result, partnership firms face problems in expansion beyond a certain size.

(iii) Possibility of conflicts:

A partnership is run by a group of persons wherein the decision-making authority is shared. Differences in opinion on the same issues may lead to disputes between partners. Further, the decisions of one partner are binding on other partners. Thus, an unwise decision by some may result in financial ruin for all. In case a partner desires to leave the firm, this can result in the termination of the partnership as there is a restriction on transfer of ownership.

(iv) Lack of continuity:

A partnership can come to an end due to the following cases: death, retirement or insolvency of any partner. This may result in a lack of continuity. However, the remaining partners can enter into a fresh agreement and continue to run the business.

(v) Lack of public confidence:

A partnership firm is not legally required to publish its financial reports or make other related information public. Hence, it is difficult for members of the public to ascertain the financial status of a partnership firm. As a result, the confidence of the public in partnership firms is generally low.

(Source: NCERT – Business Studies, Class XI)

The Memory Solution:

To memorize the points of this long answer, let's imagine a situation in which three friends who had gone to study at a premium management institute decide to rent an apartment in partnership and live together. Now let's visualize all the merits and demerits of partnership in this situation.

MERITS:

i) **Ease of formation and closure:**

Let's imagine that it was very easy for the three friends to live together. They put in some personal money and rented the apartment. They agreed to move out and live separately too, in case one individual wants to.

ii) **Balanced decision-making:**

Each friend made decisions for the house based on his area of knowledge. For example, one decided what fruits and vegetables to buy for meals. The second decided which dishes needed to be cooked. This reduced the burden on just one person to shop and plan all meals.

iii) **More funds:**

When the three people lived together, each would contribute more money from their pockets for the affairs of the household.

iv) **Sharing of risks:**

All three friends bore the risks collectively. Whatever problem took place in the house, they collectively tackled it.

v) **Secrecy:**

The friends made a pact that whatever discussions, arguments or private conversations they would have between themselves would not be known to anyone outside of their house. Hence, no outsider would get to know anything.

LIMITATIONS:

i) **Unlimited liability:**
    The three friends had to face all their problems collectively. For example, if one friend was unable to contribute his share of the rent, then the other two were liable to pay more rent from their personal savings.

ii) **Limited resources:**
    As the three friends lived in a small house, not a lot of people could come to visit or stay. The money that each contributed remained limited, and so they could not think of buying luxurious items for the house.

iii) **Possibility of conflicts:**
    The three friends lived together, but they often had different opinions on the same situation. This increased the possibility of conflict among the three.

iv) **Lack of continuity:**
    If, due to any problem, one of the friends decided to leave, the other two would have to leave too, or otherwise they would have to share the rent and responsibilities between them. Only then would they be able to continue to be together.

v) **Lack of public confidence:**
    As the three friends lived alone without their families and did not reveal much about the affairs of the house, the other people living in their apartment complex did not have confidence in them.

We are sure that memorizing the points with the help of scenarios makes it easier. Similarly, you can imagine a real-life joint family from your life to memorize points related to joint-family business, or your parent running a sole-ownership business to memorize the related points. This will help you recall points quickly, as only the related points will come to your mind, thus removing any confusion.

IX. HOW TO REVISE

CHAPTER 40

★★★

SCIENTIFIC REVISION PLAN

It has often been observed that even after putting in a lot of hard work throughout the year and memorizing the whole syllabus, students find that they forget the prepared content (or answers) as soon as exams approach. This makes them believe that there is no use in preparing for exams in advance as they are eventually going to forget all the important content. So they prefer preparing in the last few days before the exams, thus leading to stress. All this happens because students miss one thing in their planning: a proper revision plan that can give them their desired result.

★★★ SCIENTIFIC REVISION PLAN ★★★

Let us present a revision plan that will help you retain information for a long time. To understand this plan, you need to understand how any piece of information is retained in our memory.

Whatever you learn first goes into your short-term memory; when you revise it, it shifts to your long-term memory. The catch here is when you revise a topic. Suppose you have studied a topic a month before the exam, and you plan to revise it just before the exam—you will, most likely, forget it by then and will have to exert more effort again.

This is because our brain can retain any new information correctly only for the first twenty-four hours. After that, our first *forgetting cycle* begins, and we start forgetting. So it is important that the **first revision** should be done **within the first twenty-four hours** after you have learnt a new topic.

This revision will help you keep that information in your brain for the next seven days, and by then your second forgetting cycle will begin. So your **second revision** should be done **within the next seven days**. This can be followed by a monthly or bi-monthly revision, depending on the difficulty of the topic.

Now, the first thought that might come to your mind is 'Who has the time to follow this revision schedule?'

Just think about it, though. Let's say you took two hours, i.e., 120 minutes, to memorize a topic for the first time. When you revise it in the first twenty-four hours, do you think it will take you as much time? *No.*

Revision takes about one-tenth of the first learning time, as you already know the content. So it will hardly take 10-12 minutes, or even less, to revise it in the next seven days and then monthly. Once you start following this revision plan, you will realize that you are able to remember the information over a long period of time, and that too with absolute accuracy.

Now let's see what happens if you are not able to follow this revision plan due to a lack of time.

Let's assume that you memorized a chapter from a particular subject thoroughly, made memory notes and associations, and are confident that you will remember it till the time of the exam without needing revision. But as you didn't revise in the first twenty-four hours, your first forgetting cycle starts. One week passes without revision, and your second forgetting cycle starts.

Every day you are memorizing more information from different subjects of your syllabus, without going back to previous chapters. One month passes without revision or looking at your notes.

Now after two months, the exam is just around the corner and you have already prepared ten out of twelve chapters in the last two months. You are confident that you will score well, as ten chapters have been thoroughly prepared and only two chapters are remaining, for which you have enough time to cover.

What do you think? Will you be able to recall all those chapters that you studied initially but did not revise?
Will you be able to recall all the information or some part of it?

Well, studies show that you will be able to retain only 5 to 7 per cent of the information. The rest will be forgotten.

The result: panic and stress!

You feel worthless and doubt your memory. All your hard work seems to have gone down the drain. You are neither able to revise the chapter previously studied, as it will now take a lot of time, nor able to study the remaining chapters. These negative thoughts just before the exams will weaken your confidence and will affect your overall performance.

That is why we emphasize that **you must understand the importance of revision on a regular basis and in a scientific manner**, as has been explained here. We can say through our experience with many students who plan their study schedule and periodic revision that they become more organized and calmer before the exams and perform exceptionally well. Revision done with visualization makes it that much easier.

★★★ THE BEST TIME TO REVISE ★★★

When we sleep at night, our body is at rest but our brain is busy organizing the information we have taken in throughout the day, especially the things that are on our mind just before sleeping. So if you revise the information you memorized during the day just **one hour** before you sleep, you will be able to cover ten times more than you normally would.

This is what we call smart work, where knowing the right technique helps you achieve more in less time and with less effort.

This is the objective of writing this book: to help students learn smart techniques of memorizing and scheduling their revision, so as to enable them to explore the immense potential of their memory and add this smart work to their hard work, resulting in unparalleled academic success.

APPENDIX

THE POWER OF VISUALIZATION

While going through the memory techniques taught in this book, you must have identified a common element that is present throughout the chapters: *creative visualization*. Visualization not only plays a vital role in enhancing memory but also helps you make your dreams and goals come true. Let us share with you an amazing story related to this.

Bill Gates, best known as one of the richest people on the planet, is the co-founder of Microsoft Corporation, which is one of the world's largest software companies. He is also an author and a philanthropist, running the Bill and Melinda Gates Foundation, the largest private foundation in the world.

When Bill Gates was only twenty years old, he told his colleagues, 'When I am thirty years old, I will become a millionaire and I will put a computer in every home.'

At that time, he was just a young software developer on a leave of absence from college to start his own software company. People laughed at his dream, as computers back then were only used as a gaming tool. But Gates followed his dream; he worked hard with determination and patience, working for more than sixteen hours a day! He *visualized* himself as a millionaire, but **at thirty-one he became the youngest billionaire ever** and **at thirty-nine he was the richest man on earth!**

How did he achieve so much?

It was surely his hard work along with consistent positive thinking and visualization of his future success that helped him achieve his goal so fast.

Through this story we learn that thoughts play a very important role in the journey of your life. The way you think makes your body respond in a similar pattern. Through your thoughts, you programme your brain to release chemicals and hormones that help you accomplish the task accordingly. If you **create positive thoughts**, such as believing you can do it, your brain immediately accepts this and releases hormones that support this thought. You **start getting the right ideas** in your mind, and your body starts responding in favour of your thoughts, which helps you achieve your target.

But when you start thinking negatively, like **doubting yourself** or thinking that you can't do something because it is difficult or impossible, your brain accepts these thoughts and releases hormones and chemicals accordingly, which increase your body's resistance to accomplishing that task. This further **withdraws energy from your body** and doesn't let you achieve your target. Hence, you must learn to master your mind by controlling your thoughts.

A very popular quote by the Buddha goes: **'The mind is everything. What you think, you become.'**

To understand this, let's talk about a real-life experiment. A few athletes were made to sit comfortably on a chair and were asked to visualize themselves running on a race track. At the same time, their brainwaves, pulse rate, muscle tone and heartbeat were monitored using biofeedback machines. After analysing the results of the test, it was found that the athletes' muscles, heart rate and brainwaves were all responding as if the athletes were *actually* running on the track.

How could this be possible?

This was because the brain could not make out if the athletes were running on the track in reality or just visualizing it in their mind. It responds in the same manner in both situations. So, along with the physical effort, if you visualize success in your mind, it programmes your brain and thereby your body to perform in the desired way.

This science of the brain is being used by athletes all over the world to train their mind and body before their actual performance on the field. They visualize each and every moment of their performance in an extremely detailed way.

Visualizing an event, situation or object attracts it to your life. All successful people use it consciously or unconsciously, by visualizing their goals clearly and then seeing themselves accomplish these goals.

Visualization plays a very crucial role in our formative years, when we are building a foundation for our future. As a student you must see your goals clearly in your mind and imagine yourself achieving those goals.

Henry Ford once said, '**Whether you think you can or think you can't—you're right.**'

This is absolutely true, as the brain follows what you think. But the truth is that whenever we are presented with a challenge, the first thought that comes to our mind is of failure, as we doubt our capabilities. Negative thoughts cloud our mind and remind us of our previous failures. To tackle this unwanted development, you must understand the following analogy.

Let's say the road to your goal has four steps; your determination, consistent hard work and smart skills will take you three steps ahead. But before that fourth step you have to visualize yourself as successful, and only then will you reach your goal. Any negative thoughts will pull you one step back and slowly take you away from your aim. On the contrary, after all the hard work and smart skills, if you visualize your goal with positivity, your speed of moving towards your target will increase manifold, and you will be able to achieve your goal even before your stipulated time, just like Bill Gates did.

★★★ GETTING RID OF NEGATIVE THOUGHTS ★★★

We would like to ask you a simple question:

If there is complete darkness in a room, how will you remove that darkness?

The answer is simple, isn't it?

You just turn on the lights.

This is exactly what we have to do with our thoughts. We are sure you will agree when we say that there is no such thing as darkness; it's just the absence of light. Similarly, negative thoughts do not exist. It's just the absence of positive thoughts. When our mind is full of fear, we feel incapable of moving ahead and lose our focus. At that time it becomes important to gain control of our mind. Instead of thinking about the things you cannot do, think about what you *can* achieve. You should always **visualize** yourself as a **winner**. Bill Gates didn't say he *wanted* to be a millionaire at thirty; he said he *will be*. He always imagined himself as achieving the target. You should follow the same. All your efforts should be focused on creating more positive thoughts instead of stopping the negative ones. Think of how you will perform the task at hand

and complete it successfully. Visualize yourself being appreciated and rewarded. Imagine celebrating your success. All these positive thoughts will take you on the passage to success. Whatever you visualize, you will actualize, as your brain will respond that way. This visualization will increase your confidence, and you will be able to face challenges with energy and vigour.

With this new-found knowledge, embark on a journey of positivity and imagine yourself reaching incredible heights.

We wish you all the best!

ACKNOWLEDGEMENTS

'ALONE WE CAN DO SO LITTLE; TOGETHER WE CAN DO SO MUCH'—HELEN KELLER

This quotation holds true for this book, as it is an outcome of not just our efforts but also the encouragement, unbiased feedback and unparalleled support of many people.

Our first thanks go to the Almighty God for bestowing upon us wisdom and for giving us the opportunity to share our knowledge with other people.

The readers of our earlier books deserve a big thanks, as their constant feedback about the help they are getting from those books inspired us to come up with and write this book.

We would also like to thank our students and all the teachers who were a part of our numerous workshops; their ideas helped us work out many of the memory solutions given in this book.

We would also like to thank our family; M. Saquib, our illustrator; our friend Jaya Kalwani; and, finally, our editors, Sohini Mitra and Arpita Nath, along with the entire Penguin Random House team. Their unwavering support throughout the making of this book helped give it its present shape, which is better than we ever imagined.